Staging Violence Against Women and Girls

T0283576

Staging Violence Against Women and Girls

Plays and Interviews

Edited by

DANIELA CAVALLARO, LUCIANA D'ARCANGELI
and CLAIRE KENNEDY

methuen | drama

LONDON · NEW YORK · OXFORD · NEW DELHI · SYDNEY

METHUEN DRAMA
Bloomsbury Publishing Plc
50 Bedford Square, London, WC1B 3DP, UK
1385 Broadway, New York, NY 10018, USA
29 Earlsfort Terrace, Dublin 2, Ireland

BLOOMSBURY, METHUEN DRAMA and the Methuen Drama logo are
trademarks of Bloomsbury Publishing Plc

First published in Great Britain 2023

Copyright © Daniela Cavallaro, Luciana d'Arcangeli and Claire Kennedy, 2023
Sleight of Hand © Isley Lynn, 2023
Where Do I Start? © Raúl Quirós Molina, 2023
Dancing Feet © Bahar Brunton, 2023
Mutant © Karis E. Halsall, 2023
Interview with Melissa Dean and Alex Crampton © Daniela Cavallaro and Claire Kennedy, 2023
Interviews with the authors of *Little Stitches* © Daniela Cavallaro, 2023
'Kubra' © Dacia Maraini, 2023
Translation of 'Kubra' © Sharon Wood, 2023
Interview with Dacia Maraini © Luciana d'Arcangeli, 2023
Translation of Interview with Dacia Maraini © Luciana d'Arcangeli, 2023
Interview with Nicolette Kay and further reflection by Olivia Brown © Claire Kennedy, 2023
Interview with Ainsley Burdell © Claire Kennedy, 2023
A Trial for Rape © adapted by Renato Chiocca from the documentary *Processo per stupro* by Maria Grazia
Belmonti, Anna Carini, Rony Daopoulo, Paola De Martiis, Annabella Miscuglio and Loredana Rotondo, 2023
Translation of *A Trial for Rape* © Claire Kennedy, 2023
Interview with Renato Chiocca © Daniela Cavallaro, 2023
Translation of Interview with Renato Chiocca © Claire Kennedy, 2023

The authors have asserted their right under the Copyright, Designs and Patents Act, 1988,
to be identified as authors of this work.

For legal purposes the Acknowledgements on pp. xii–xiii constitute an extension of this copyright page.

Cover design: Rebecca Heselton
Cover image © Lucienne Fontannaz

All rights reserved. No part of this publication may be reproduced or transmitted in any form or by any means,
electronic or mechanical, including photocopying, recording, or any information storage or retrieval system,
without prior permission in writing from the publishers.

Bloomsbury Publishing Plc does not have any control over, or responsibility for, any third-party websites
referred to in this book. All internet addresses given in this book were correct at the time of going to press. The
authors and publisher regret any inconvenience caused if addresses have changed or sites have ceased to
exist, but can accept no responsibility for any such changes.

No rights in incidental music or songs contained in the work are hereby granted and performance rights for any
performance/presentation whatsoever must be obtained from the respective copyright owners.
All rights whatsoever regarding the plays in this book are strictly reserved and application for performance etc.
should be made before rehearsals by professionals and by amateurs to:
Melissa Dean, melissadean88@googlemail.com for *Little Stitches*, Nicolette Kay, New Shoes Theatre,
nicolette@newshoestheatre.org.uk for 'Kubra', Renato Chiocca, renatochiocca@hotmail.com for *A Trial for Rape*.

A catalogue record for this book is available from the British Library.

A catalog record for this book is available from the Library of Congress.

ISBN: HB: 978-1-3503-2971-3
         PB: 978-1-3503-2970-6
         ePDF: 978-1-3503-2973-7
         eBook: 978-1-3503-2972-0

Series: Methuen Drama Play Collections

Typeset by RefineCatch Limited, Bungay, Suffolk
Printed and bound in Great Britain

To find out more about our authors and books visit www.bloomsbury.com
and sign up for our newsletters.

*The work of the artists in this book invites us all
to continue the struggle to eliminate violence against women and girls,
whether through theatre or other means,
for a better future for all.*

Claire, Daniela, Luciana

Contents

Figures

Contributors

Little Stitches

Bahar Brunton grew up in London. In addition to *Dancing Feet*, she has had two plays produced: *The Highwayman*, at the Battersea Barge and the Edinburgh Festival in 2008; and *Sofka*, at the Calder Bookshop & Theatre in 2012 and 2013. Her stories have been published by Fairlight Books, *Firewords* magazine, *The Frogmore Papers* and Ether Books.

Alex Crampton is an artist and educator. Passionate about systemic change, her work is devoted to ecological, spiritual and social regeneration. She uses theatre, illustration and ceremony to empower others in their unique self-expression and amplify world-changing stories. As an award-winning theatre director, producer, dramaturg and educational practitioner she has worked with the Donmar Warehouse, Gate Theatre, Almeida Theatre, Soho Theatre, Southwark Playhouse, Arcola Theatre, RIFT and Blind Summit. She is based in west Wales.

Melissa Dean is an actress, writer, producer and radio presenter, who uses her creativity as a means for activism. Since 2010, she has appeared in TV series such as *Line of Duty*, *Doctors* and *EastEnders*. She co-starred in *Me You Us Them*, which explores stories of race and belonging in Northern Ireland, staged by Terra Nova Productions in 2018 and filmed for online distribution in 2022. She has a talk show on Reform Radio, called 'A Safe Space to Articulate', which looks into unhealthy attitudes and stories in and around the arts, with the aim of helping create a healthier workspace. She is the first Artist in Residence at Reform Radio and works with the *Guardian* providing voice-over for podcast reads.

Karis E. Halsall has been writing for theatre for the last decade, working with acclaimed companies such as the Hampstead Theatre, Theatre503, HighTide Festival, Headlong, the Bush Theatre, DryWrite and Nabokov. Following her recent transition into writing for the screen, her inaugural short film *Period Piece* was selected to screen internationally at prestigious female-centric festivals including the Underwire Film Festival (2018) and Vancouver International Women in Film Festival (2019). Her television credits include BBC Three.

Isley Lynn's play *Skin a Cat* was awarded Pick of the Year at the Vault Festival 2016 and its production at The Bunker later that year led to four nominations for Off West End Awards including Most Promising New Playwright and Best New Play; it then toured nationally in 2018. Other credits include: *The War of the Worlds* (New Diorama Theatre 2019, international tour 2021); 'Canace' in *15 Heroines* (Jermyn Street Theatre 2020); *Albatross* (Paines Plough and the Royal Welsh College of Music and Drama at Bute Theatre and Gate Theatre 2018); *The Swell* (HighTide First Commissions play reading 2018); *Sie und Wir* (Us and Them) for Werk X in Vienna (2016); *Tether* (Edinburgh Fringe Festival 2015); and *What's So Special* (as part of The Get Out at the Royal Court Jerwood Theatre Upstairs 2014). Her play *Bright Nights* was a Script6 winner at The Space in 2014. Isley was a finalist for the 2021 Women's Prize for Playwriting.

Raúl Quirós Molina has an MA in Creative Writing from City, University of London. His plays include *The Dinner*, produced at the Vault Festival (London 2015), and *El pan y la sal* (Bread and Salt) at the Teatro Español (Madrid 2018), in addition to *Where Do I Start?* He was a finalist for the Nadal Novel Prize in 2018 and was awarded the Felipe Trigo Novel Prize in 2019 for *Los caballos inocentes* (The Innocent Horses). He currently lives and works in Barcelona.

'Kubra'

Olivia Brown graduated from the National Institute of Dramatic Art in Sydney in 1969 and since then has worked as an actor in theatre, television, film and radio, and independently as a director, writer, producer and theatre educator. From 1985 to 1992 she managed her own theatre company which operated in schools and community venues throughout New South Wales (NSW). She has engaged in a number of creative partnerships, most notably when working with the Italian Institute of Culture (Sydney), SBS TV and CARNIVALE (NSW Multicultural Arts Festival) on bilingual productions of Dacia Maraini's play *Maria Stuarda* (Mary Stuart) for stage (Wharf Theatre 2) and television.

Ainsley Burdell is a director, performer and teacher who has worked in the arts and community cultural development in Queensland over the past thirty years. She has engaged with a wide range of communities involving unionist, youth, immigrant and women's groups, to develop and produce theatre works that express their stories and experiences.

Nicolette Kay has directed and co-translated a number of plays by Dacia Maraini as well as contributing to books about the playwright. She gave a talk about directing Maraini's *Hurried Steps* at TEDx CoventGardenWomen, called 'Hidden Stories, Hurried Steps'. She is the Artistic Director of New Shoes Theatre and has directed and toured professional productions in diverse venues in the UK and Sydney as well as directing students at the Birmingham Conservatoire. She trained as an actress at the Drama Centre London, worked with the Women's Theatre Group and has played leading roles with the Cambridge Theatre Company, Gate Theatre and Young Vic Theatre in London, and in repertory theatres across the UK.

Dacia Maraini is one of the most widely read Italian writers in the world. While the subject matter of her novels, short stories, plays, screenplays, poetry, essays and interviews covers a broad range, her focus is always on women's condition. She is also a theatre and cinema director, who has founded or collaborated with various experimental companies. Among her numerous literary awards are the Premio Strega in 1999 for the short story collection *Buio* (Darkness; 2002 in English), the Premio Campiello in 1990 for the novel *La lunga vita di Marianna Ucrìa* (The Silent Duchess; 1992 in English) and the Premio Campiello again in 2012 for her career. She was a finalist for the 2011 Man Booker International Prize and nominated for the 2012 Nobel Prize in Literature. Further testimony to the impact of her work around the world are eight honorary degrees – from the universities of Naples 'L'Orientale', Macerata, L'Aquila, Foggia and Bucharest, Middlebury College (Vermont), John Cabot University (Rome) and Chapman University (California) – the Japanese Order of the Rising Sun, conferred in 2017, and the highest Italian honour, the Knight Grand Cross, awarded in 1996.

Sharon Wood is Professor (Emerita) at the University of Leicester and the author and editor of numerous books on writing by women in Italy. She has published several translations, including works by Primo Levi, Romana Petri, Gabriella Maleti, Susanna Tamaro and Dacia Maraini.

A Trial for Rape

Renato Chiocca is a director and screenwriter who works in cinema, theatre and television. He is also co-author, with Andrea Ferraris, of the graphic novel *The Scar: Graphic reportage from the U.S.–Mexico border* (2019), also released in Italy, France, Portugal, Spain and Latin America.

Editors

Daniela Cavallaro is an honorary research academic at the University of Auckland. Her publications include *Italian Women's Theatre 1930–1960: An anthology of plays* (2011) and *Educational Theatre for Women in Post-World War II Italy: A stage of their own* (2017).

Luciana d'Arcangeli recently left Flinders University, Adelaide, where she taught Italian theatre, cinema and translation as Cassamarca Senior Lecturer. Author of *I personaggi femminili nel teatro di Dario Fo e Franca Rame* (2009), she has also published widely in journals and edited several books and special journal issues on Italian cinema and theatre. Among her awards are the Italia nel Mondo prize (2016), a gold medal from the Dante Alighieri Society (2017) and the Prize for Italian Literary Translation (2018) from the Italian Institute of Culture in Melbourne. She is currently an adjunct professor, language consultant, translator and interpreter, based in Rome.

Claire Kennedy is an adjunct senior lecturer at Griffith University, Brisbane, where she previously taught Italian language and contemporary history. She has published widely on language pedagogy, co-edited special journal issues on Italians in Australia, and translated and subtitled several plays for performance. With Daniela Cavallaro and Luciana d'Arcangeli she co-edited *Atti di accusa: Testi teatrali e interviste sulla rappresentazione della violenza contro le donne* (2021), which contains Italian versions of the plays in this book.

Acknowledgements

Our very warm thanks go to:

the authors who provided their plays for publication in this book and patiently answered our various questions about them: Isley Lynn, Raúl Quirós Molina, Bahar Brunton and Karis E. Halsall for *Little Stitches*; Dacia Maraini for 'Kubra'; Renato Chiocca for *Processo per stupro* (A Trial for Rape);

Sharon Wood for permission to publish her translation of 'Kubra';

the directors and producers of these plays for their insights and the time they have dedicated to our interview questions on their productions: Alex Crampton and Melissa Dean for *Little Stitches*; Nicolette Kay, Olivia Brown and Ainsley Burdell for 'Kubra'; and Renato Chiocca for *Processo per stupro*;

Lucienne Fontannaz for providing her artwork 'The Tear' (2014) for reproduction on the book cover;

the photographers for permission to use their images: John Wilson and Justin Jones for images from performances of *Little Stitches* in London in 2014 and 2015 respectively; Geoff Sirmai, director of Sirmai Arts Marketing (www.sirmai.com.au) for images of 'Kubra' in the Sydney production of *Hurried Steps* in 2016; Federica Di Benedetto for images from *Processo per stupro* staged at the Teatro Eliseo in Rome in 2018;

Tim Page (University of Auckland) for his expertise and patience in retrieving and converting images;

the scholars who assisted with terminology on FGM/C: Laura Lori and Juliet Rogers (University of Melbourne); and Lucrezia Catania, medical specialist and researcher (Referral Centre for Curing and Preventing FGM, AOUC – Careggi University Hospital, Florence);

the late Gaye Wilkinson for some valuable insights in her unpublished translation of *Processo per stupro*;

our colleagues Giorgia Alù (University of Sydney) and Laura Peja (Università Cattolica) who contributed questions and observations for the interview with Dacia Maraini;

the participants in the conference Indelible (Eng.) / *Indelebile* (It.) – Representation in the Arts of (In)visible Violence Against Women and Their Resistance (Adelaide, 23–5 October 2019), and the creative artists who provided live music and theatre as part of the conference programme, all of whom contributed to intense and inspiring discussion on the theme;

the Australasian Centre for Italian Studies (ACIS), and in particular its Chairs, David Moss and Catherine Kovesi, for their commitment to the Visual and Performance Studies (VPS) research group of 2018–20, whose aims are set out at https://www.acis. org.au/research, and our fellow VPS group members Giorgia Alù (University of Sydney) and Sally Hill (Victoria University of Wellington). The ACIS sponsorship and support allowed us to work together to organize the 'Indelible' conference and publish this book and other academic works;

and our loved ones for their constant emotional and professional support.

Daniela Cavallaro, Luciana d'Arcangeli and Claire Kennedy

About the cover image

'The Tear' by Lucienne Fontannaz © Lucienne Fontannaz 2014. Reproduced with the permission of the artist.

'The Tear' was created by the layering of images from current popular magazines. Appropriation, and the use of collage as a medium, in black and white, facilitated direct physical and conceptual links to the subject matter. Violence against women leaves them mutilated, their bodies, minds and hearts like emptied vessels, wrecked upon the shore of individuality and relationships. In this image, little appears to remain of the woman's slumped body, just some skin and hair, likely not enough material to sew together in repair.

Lucienne Fontannaz

Lucienne Fontannaz is originally from Switzerland and now lives in Australia. 'The Tear' is one of a series of images created during a Master by Research in Fine Arts, in 2014 (see Fontannaz 2022). Lucienne completed a Doctor of Visual Arts in 2021, in which she explored the demise of female archetypes. Over the past decade, her artworks have addressed objectification and the stereotypical portrayals of the female body, sexuality and pornography, historically and in the present.

Introduction: The stories behind the statistics

The arts can make visible the often invisible, and yet indelible, acts of violence perpetrated every day against women and girls (VAWG), and highlight the urgency of action towards its elimination. They are instrumental in exposing the complexity of the numerous forms that VAWG can take in the contemporary world, as well as exploring new and old possibilities for resistance. Our research project in this field[1] has sought to contribute to the 'glocal' conversation on the topic and, at the same time, raise awareness of the global extent of the problem and the fundamental role of the arts in making us see, or re-see, what is otherwise familiar, 'normal' and invisible. The plays in this book are some of the works we have collected and discussed in the project: *Little Stitches*, comprising four short plays by Isley Lynn, Raúl Quirós Molina, Bahar Brunton and Karis E. Halsall, first performed in London in 2014; 'Kubra', a section added by Dacia Maraini to her play *Hurried Steps* for its production in Sydney in 2016; and *A Trial for Rape*, translated from the Italian *Processo per stupro*, created by Renato Chiocca and first performed in Rome in 2018.[2] *Little Stitches* and 'Kubra' share a thematic focus in that they denounce in particular the violence operated on girls and women by the practices of female genital modification/ cutting (FGM/C).[3] 'Kubra' and *A Trial for Rape* share a courtroom setting and the scenario of a woman survivor seeking justice – not in the sense of punishment of those who have harmed them, but in the sense of change in society's understanding of what has been done to them, and change in the institutions and processes for dealing with it.

Staging Violence Against Women and Girls sits between anthologies of plays and scholarly analyses, and is aimed at both theatre practitioners and academics from various disciplines. The plays are accompanied by interviews with their authors, directors and producers, which, together with this Introduction, are intended to situate the texts and their productions in context. In bringing together academic and creative work, we seek to provide a sort of community of practice to facilitate and encourage further productions of these plays, with the goal of raising awareness of the types of VAWG they address.

---

1 This book is one of the research outputs of the project titled Indelible (Eng.) / *Indelebile* (It.): The Representation of (In)visible Violence Against Women and Their Resistance, carried out by the Visual and Performance Studies (VPS) Research Group sponsored by the Australasian Centre for Italian Studies (ACIS) from 2018 to 2022. See https://www.acis.org.au/research for summary information on the project, and the appendix to d'Arcangeli and Kennedy (2022) for other outputs.

2 Prior to this book, we published the same collection of plays in Italian, under the title *Atti di accusa: Testi teatrali e interviste sulla rappresentazione della violenza contro le donne* (Cavallaro, d'Arcangeli and Kennedy 2021).

3 These practices are often defined in legal and policy documents as female genital mutilation (FGM), but many survivors prefer the label female genital modification or female genital cutting (FGC). In this Introduction we adopt the abbreviation used in UNICEF documents: FGM/C (see UNICEF 2016) and for ourselves interpret the 'M' as 'modification'. See the Human Rights Watch (2010) site for a brief overview of acronyms and terms used, and the World Health Organization fact sheet for a description of the different types of FGM/C (WHO 2022). We have not standardized naming of the practices throughout the rest of this book; that is, we have left each interviewee's use of labels as is, and naturally have not made any changes to the writers' wording in the playscripts.

The statistics on VAWG around the world are staggering: every two seconds a girl under eighteen is married; 35 per cent of women (one sixth of the entire world population) have been sexually assaulted, mostly by an intimate partner; and the figure of 81,000 femicides reported for 2020 amounts to 'a woman or girl being killed every 11 minutes in their home' (UN Office on Drugs and Crime 2021). And this is despite significant recent advances in laws and procedures in many countries.[4] Dacia Maraini, in her interview, likens this scenario of human rights violation to a war.

The plays in this book go beyond the numbers to tell some individual stories of violence – against women and girls named Dunya, Felicity, Safa, Kubra and Fiorella, and others, unnamed. The stories of these women and girls, and their communities, touch us in a different way from even the most alarming statistics. Plays such as these give human form to the definition of VAWG in the UN Declaration on the Elimination of Violence Against Women: 'any act of gender-based violence that results in, or is likely to result in, physical, sexual, or psychological harm or suffering to women, including threats of such acts, coercion or arbitrary deprivation of liberty, whether occurring in public or in private life' (UN WOMEN n. d.).

Such stories can move us, and urge us to act for change. But in what ways can theatre be expected to achieve social change? Emma Willis (2021: 2) quotes Joanne Tompkins (2014: 29) as acknowledging that theatre 'almost never has [the] capacity' to create political change directly, but arguing that 'it is possible that a performance might affect audiences significantly by demonstrating how change for the social good (however incremental) might take place off the stage'. One important study in this area is Lisa Fitzpatrick's *Rape on the Contemporary Stage* (2018), in which she sets out to 'identify a politics and practice of rape prevention that can emerge from the transformative potential of theatrical performance' (33). She finds cause for optimism in the 'dialogue with the audience and society' that has been developed over thirty years by women theatre-makers, a process she sees as not only raising awareness but shifting beliefs towards 'an understanding of rape as an act of violence' (253). And with respect to FGM/C in particular, theatre has already proved to be a powerful tool for social change, because it affects understanding and emotions (UNFPA Arab States 2018).

At the same time, all three plays in this book point to the limits on what can be obtained through law and justice systems, and indeed on what should be expected of them. The role of courts and other institutions is an important area for reflection, especially if we consider that the Convention on Preventing and Combating Violence Against Women and Domestic Violence (Council of Europe 2011)[5] includes 'punishing the perpetrators' in its priorities alongside 'preventing the violence' and 'protecting the victims'. For example, Kubra's story and the stories of Dunya, Felicity and Safa in *Little Stitches* demand that we consider the implications of punishing perpetrators of FGM/C, who often include parents of the child victim/survivors, and that we broaden the horizon of action to education and communication.

---

4 The World Bank (2022) report 'Women, Business and the Law 2022' found 160 'economies' to have laws on domestic violence, and 144 to have laws on sexual harassment in the workplace, out of the 190 considered. See also previous annual reports with the same title.

5 On 21 July 2022 the United Kingdom became the thirty-seventh State to ratify the Convention, to come into force there on 1 November 2022.

Most importantly, all three works are based on true stories and each draws either substantially or entirely on the words of real people. Raúl Quirós Molina's *Where Do I Start?*, in *Little Stitches*, is defined as verbatim theatre, and *A Trial for Rape* is adapted from the transcript of the video recording of a trial. 'Kubra' and the other component plays of *Little Stitches* also grew out of research collecting the oral or written testimony of survivors of abuse, as their creators explain in their interviews. *Little Stitches* and *Hurried Steps* are intended to be performed in conjunction with discussion and community outreach activities, and a *Trial for Rape* also lends itself to such an approach.

While working on this project through the coronavirus pandemic emergency, the closure of borders, and the escalation of armed conflict in old and new wars, we have been constantly reminded of the renewed urgency of combating VAWG. The increase in such violence around the world, in conditions of economic uncertainty, isolation and reduced mobility, was described as a 'shadow pandemic' in a UN report, which went on to note that 'In addition to exacerbating violence and inequalities, the Covid-19 pandemic [was] jeopardizing the progress achieved so far in the elimination of violence against women and girls' (United Nations General Assembly 2020: 2–3).[6]

At the same time, we felt a heightened awareness of the importance that theatre has in many people's lives. The arts sector was financially devastated in Australasia (home to all three of us at the time), as elsewhere, by the closure of theatres and cinemas, but millions of people around the world tuned in for streamed live performances, while small groups of friends opted for a do-it-yourself solution of collective online play-reading. Orchestras, choirs and other creative group activities were re-created online. Theatre in the time of Covid-19 may have been a virtual theatre, to be enjoyed online or to be read (as perhaps in this book), but it conserved the spirit of engagement and personal involvement that theatre has always embodied.

The plays

Little Stitches

This work brings together four one-act plays concerning FGM/C, by four different authors. The title makes direct reference to forms of FGM/C that include not just cutting but sewing and, as one reviewer wrote, the four pieces are also 'little stitches in themselves, coming together to create a greater patchwork or tapestry of information' (Healey 2015). The creators aimed to 'explore the human stories behind the statistics'

---

6 Plan International, which works worldwide for children's rights, also warned in May 2020 of a likely 'shadow pandemic of gender-based violence' – including increased rates of child marriage and pregnancy, with projections based on prior experience of increased teenage pregnancy and maternal mortality rates when schools had been closed during the Ebola crisis of 2014–16 (Plan International 2020b). The organization also raised the alarm specifically about an increase in the practice of FGM/C, reporting that, during lockdown in Somalia, cutters seeking business amid the economic downturn were going door-to-door to offer their services while students were home from school (Plan International 2020a).

(Arcola Theatre 2014), drawing on research that centred on oral and written testimony of FGM/C survivors.[7]

The WHO fact sheet on 'Female genital mutilation' defines it as 'compris[ing] all procedures that involve partial or total removal of the external female genitalia, or other injury to the female genital organs for non-medical reasons'. Immediate complications of these procedures include severe pain, excessive bleeding, fever, infections, shock, even death. Long-term consequences include urinary, vaginal and menstrual problems, pain during intercourse, increased risk of childbirth complications and newborn deaths, as well as psychological problems such as depression, anxiety, post-traumatic stress disorder and low self-esteem. The practice therefore 'constitutes an extreme form of discrimination against girls and women [. . .] and is a violation of the rights of children' (WHO 2022).

The data on FGM/C make clear that it is an immense global problem. The WHO fact sheet summarizes its extent early in 2022 as follows: 'more than 200 million girls and women alive today have been subjected to the practice with more than 3 million girls estimated to be at risk of FGM annually' (WHO 2022). Migration has spread FGM/C beyond its countries of origin – mainly in Africa but also in the Middle East and Asia – to diaspora communities, and it is now performed in ninety countries worldwide (Equality Now 2020). One of the *Little Stitches* writers, Isley Lynn, reveals in her interview that she had not realized 'how close to home the issue was' until conducting research for the play in London. She hoped that her play would cause others like herself to 'wake up to the fact that protecting vulnerable women and girls relates to everyone, in every community'.

Ten years ago, the United Nations General Assembly (2012) adopted the resolution *Intensifying Global Efforts for the Elimination of Female Genital Mutilations*. Since then, the media in many Western countries have reported more frequently on the practice and on cases that have gone to trial. It was one such newspaper report that provided the spark for *Little Stitches*, as producer Melissa Dean reveals in her interview.

In the first of the four plays, *Sleight of Hand* by Isley Lynn, we gradually learn of a girl in London, Dunya, being taken 'home' to an African country during the school holidays for a special ceremony. We meet Dunya's teacher, a postal worker, a flight attendant, an ice cream van driver and a street cleaner, all of whom realize something is wrong, as they witness different moments in Dunya's story, but dare not ask or act. *Where Do I Start?*, by Raúl Quirós Molina, begins with testimony from activists and health professionals who have worked with FGM/C survivors. It moves gradually into a monologue by Felicity, which includes memories of the day she was cut as a child, her migration as a war refugee to the UK, and her recent experience of giving talks at schools about FGM/C. Bahar Brunton's *Dancing Feet*, set in an unspecified country, is a conversation between two women who mind girls after their procedure, as they rest and recover. The women are proud to be involved in the proceedings that turn girls into 'clean' young women, while celebrations are heard in the next room, but their talk also turns to the pain and damage to their own bodies from FGM/C – and to the terminal

---

7 For a deeper analysis of these and other plays concerning FGM/C see Seguro and Tirado (2022) and Cavallaro (forthcoming).

damage to the unnamed girl they are minding. In *Mutant* by Karis E. Halsall, we are in the UK again, and Safa tells of coming home from school to the horror of a procedure in the living room, the realization of her family's betrayal and the shattering of her dreams for the future. We also hear from a Dr Chaudhry, who only a few years later attends Safa's first childbirth, and we then understand that Safa's procedure was of type III, infibulation. Dr Chaudhry admits that, when pressed by Safa's husband, he 'stitched her back up' after the birth, despite his misgivings and his empathy for his patient. He explains his decision as driven by concern that this might be carried out by others in unsafe conditions if he were to refuse.[8]

These four plays thus offer us examples of thoughts, words, deeds and failures to act, by an array of different characters, that have directly or indirectly led to acts of violence on women and girls in the form of FGM/C. They implicitly advocate for specific training for health workers and teachers, and educational measures in society broadly. The plays may be uncomfortable to watch or read, but the stories are not sensationalized. On the contrary, their creators – as they make clear in the interviews – have sought to transmit and elicit awareness and empathy, to bring the stories close to us. All performances of *Little Stitches*, both in theatres and in local libraries, were followed by post-show discussions which provided support for audience members to process the distressing material and opportunities to further explore the issues and the possibilities for effecting change.

'Kubra'

For several decades now, Dacia Maraini has investigated and denounced VAWG in her work – across fiction, drama, poetry, essays and film.[9] Yet theatre is her preferred literary form for political struggle, as she says in her interview, due to its capacity to generate a sense of community and shared responsibility. In 2004, Maraini was invited by Amnesty International to create a theatrical production as part of its international campaign against VAWG. From among the wealth of material provided to her by Amnesty, Maraini adapted, amalgamated and dramatized seven stories set in different parts of the world, which were first staged in Rome in 2005 and published in Italy in 2007 under the title *Passi affrettati* (*Hurried Steps*).[10] The title comes from the account given by two Jordanian teenagers, in one of those stories, of their daily routine of taking their sheep to graze every morning: 'we have to walk fast, with hurried steps, never looking up from the ground. Once we reach the pasture we can raise our eyes, there's no one to watch us there' (Maraini 2013: 15). The author also used this image to describe the situation of women trying to escape violent home environments: 'With hurried steps these women flee from pain and discrimination. But all too often these steps are halted, stopped, nailed down, made to turn back upon themselves' (11).

---

8 The first court case against a doctor in the UK under FGM/C law was in progress while the play was being written and performed. A doctor was charged in 2012, suspected of having re-infibulated a woman when stitching her post-partum. He was acquitted in 2015 (Laville 2015).

9 See Bellesia (2000), Manson (2005) and Mandolini (2018), among others, for discussion of the representation of VAWG in Maraini's work.

10 For further discussion of *Hurried Steps* see Wood (2013) and Cavallaro (2019).

Since then, when *Hurried Steps* has been performed in countries not yet 'represented' in its montage of cases, Maraini has added stories local to those productions – as is the case for 'Kubra', written in 2016 and set in Australia. The women and girls of the other stories in *Hurried Steps* are Albanian, Belgian, Italian, Mexican, Nigerian, Tibetan and Welsh, and the violence enacted upon them includes intimate partner violence (physical and psychological), rape, gang rape by soldiers, child trafficking and prostitution, execution by stoning and burning, and murder by shooting. The work now has ten sections, from which a selection can be made for any performance. All of them have been translated into English by Sharon Wood.

'Kubra' was born from the suggestion by Nicolette Kay, of New Shoes Theatre in the UK, and Olivia Brown, actor and producer in Australia, that *Hurried Steps* be staged in Sydney, with the added story to be set in that city and address FGM/C. Among the material Maraini worked with in writing 'Kubra', material compiled by Brown and Kay from extensive research, were reports on the first prosecution in New South Wales for FGM/C, in 2015. The case involved members of the Dawoodi Bohra Shia Muslim community, and the girls concerned were two sisters, aged around seven at the time. In 2016 the woman accused of carrying out the cutting and the girls' mother were convicted and given home detention, and a religious leader was found guilty of being an accessory after the fact, for having obstructed investigation into the practice of FGM/C in the community, and given a prison sentence (Safi 2016; Rogers 2019).[11] Like the other stories of *Hurried Steps*, Kubra's is based on real cases but synthesized from various sources including newspaper reports and direct testimony. The scenario is invented: Maraini places Kubra as a twenty-five-year-old in court recounting her experience of being cut as a child in the suburbs of an Australian city, in a backyard operation organized by her grandmother with her parents' consent. We learn that Kubra has reported her family members and the women who carried it out to the police and they are being investigated. Her family has disowned her.

In most *Hurried Steps* stories there are a few voices in addition to the protagonist's: there is often a narrator, and sometimes an institutional representative who comments on the situation and its significance. In the case of 'Kubra', a sympathetic barrister questions Kubra to draw out her story, and a similarly sympathetic academic provides minimal narration, while a journalist challenges them, insisting that the law is oppressing a minority, and accusing Kubra of betraying her family and culture. Maraini sets out her position on cultural relativism very clearly in her interview, and in the play gives the last word to Kubra, who explains that it is she who has been betrayed.

Maraini instructs that *Hurried Steps* must be presented in 'oratorio style', referring to the polyphonic musical compositions on semi-sacred themes originating in the Baroque period. As Kay (2013: 9) explains: 'The performers read the play from music stands in an "oratorio" style. They do not look at each other, but imagine that the person they are speaking to is in front of them. . . . [T]here are no lights or costumes to distract [the audience] from the words.' This approach reflects principles of the Theatre of the Word,

---

11 The convictions were overturned by appeal in 2018 but upheld in October 2019 by the High Court. Juliet Rogers (2019) analyses the problem at the centre of the divergence of views in the different levels of court – the question of what constitutes 'mutilation'.

which Pier Paolo Pasolini – a long-time friend and collaborator of Maraini's – defined in his 'Manifesto for a New Theatre' of 1968. His theatre was characterized by an absence of scenic action and staging, and the audience was expected to focus on hearing rather than seeing, 'in order to better understand the words spoken, *and thus the ideas, which are the real characters in this theatre* [italics in the original]' (Pasolini and Simpson 2007: 128). Furthermore, it was '*a theatre that is most of all a debate, and exchange of ideas, part of a literary and political struggle* [italics in the original]' (133). And Maraini makes a specific requirement that all *Hurried Steps* performances be followed by post-show discussion between the audience and an expert panel, and that it be allowed the same duration as the performance itself, making it an integral part of the event. The post-show forum, like the post-performance discussions after *Little Stitches*, has a twofold purpose: on one hand, the exchange of information and stories and exploration of programmes and strategies; and, on the other, the sharing and processing of emotional responses to the very confronting material.[12]

A Trial for Rape

Processo per stupro (A Trial for Rape) was staged by Renato Chiocca in 2018, forty years after the trial it portrayed, which was held in Latina, near Rome, in 1978. The trial culminated in the conviction of four men for the abduction and rape of an eighteen-year-old woman identified only as 'Fiorella', her family name being suppressed. Significant segments of the trial were recorded in the observational documentary *Processo per stupro* (A Trial for Rape) which Chiocca adapted to create the play. The documentary makers – Maria Grazia Belmonti, Anna Carini, Rony Daopoulo, Paola De Martiis, Annabella Miscuglio and Loredana Rotondo – had sought to bring to the attention of the Italian public the process by which a survivor of rape underwent what is now widely known as a 'second rape', or 'judicial rape' in court, effectively being transformed from complainant into defendant.[13] The documentary was aired twice by the Italian state television channel RAI2 in 1979 (due to public demand for a second screening), to a total audience of over 14 million. It succeeded in generating vast public discussion in Italy and is credited with being of 'major practical and symbolic significance, marking out a before and after'[14] in the development of societal attitudes regarding violation of women's rights (Buonanno 2020: 22).[15]

---

12 The *Hurried Steps* Resource Pack (Kay 2014b) provides information and instructions for companies planning productions of the play.
13 The problem persists, and not only in Italy, as is demonstrated by extensive research. For example, the systematic review by Sokratis Dinos et al. (2015) of nine research studies in the USA, Canada, UK and Germany concluded that, despite reforms in law and procedures, rape myths continued to influence jurors' decision making, with people who hold them more likely to find defendants not guilty. Chiara Federica Pedace (2017) analysed a small number of trials in Italy, in which she found that the judges' questioning tended to perpetuate stereotypes of sexual relations that see men as naturally aggressive and women as responsible for protecting their own bodies, and indeed blameworthy if they cannot.
14 In this Introduction, all translations from Italian are ours except where specified otherwise.
15 The documentary was also screened at the Museum of Modern Art in New York, where a copy is held in the archives, and won the prestigious Prix Italia international award for a TV documentary (Buonanno 2020: 20). It can be viewed on YouTube at https://www.youtube.com/watch?v=ZNvxfxZSUfI.

In 1978, when the trial of Fiorella's rapists was held, Italian law classified rape as a crime against 'public morality and decency' rather than a crime against a person – and the light sentences handed down at the end of that trial reflected the provisions of the Italian Criminal Code of the time.[16] Other laws had similarly institutionalized a patriarchal view of family and sexual relationships in Italy, and were amended by a series of legal reforms beginning in the 1970s. The mass mobilization of women in the Italian feminist movement, facilitated by increasing levels of education among women and girls, contributed fundamentally to bringing about many changes in a relatively short time span. Legal milestones that concerned family and interpersonal relations included: the 1970 divorce law (and the defeat of a referendum for its abrogation in 1974); lifting of the ban on contraceptives in 1971; reform of the Civil Code in 1975, to establish gender equality within marriage, remove the designation of a husband/father's right to use violence to discipline family members, and end discrimination against children born outside marriage; and the enactment of a law regulating abortion in 1978 (Willson 2010: 149–167). A decade after Fiorella took her abusers to court, two major decisions, by the Constitutional Court in 1987 and the Corte di Cassazione (Italy's highest court of appeal) in 1988, respectively, declared rape to violate a basic human right to sexual freedom (Lagostena Bassi 1993). Eventually, after a long period of campaigns and public debate, a new, harsher rape law was enacted in 1996 that now sees the crime in Section XII of the Criminal Code, 'Crimes against a person'.[17] Yet, as Rachel Anne Fenton (2010) argued, surveys by the Italian national statistics bureau, ISTAT, indicated that change in societal attitudes and reporting rates after the law reform was initially slow.[18] Fenton deduced that 'the symbolic recognition [in the 1996 law] of sexual autonomy [had] not had any profound effect', concluding that 'Italy still [had] a long way to go in changing its rape culture' (194).

Rape was a major concern of Italian feminists throughout the 1970s, but the immediate context of the decision to document a rape trial was defined by the heinous 'Circeo crime' of 29 September 1975 (so labelled for the locality in which it took place) and the subsequent trials. Three young men from affluent Roman families kidnapped, raped and tortured two young women, murdering one and leaving the other for dead. As their trial progressed, with extensive media coverage, the previously largely taboo topic of rape came to the centre of public discussion. Meanwhile, feminist groups had established a practice of ensuring women's presence in court for rape trials in solidarity with the complainants, as well as holding demonstrations outside, and several feminist lawyers were active in campaigns and court cases (Neonato 1992).

---

16 The Italian Criminal Code also allowed for rape charges to be extinguished in the event of a 'reparative marriage' deemed to restore the honour of the victim's family. That law was repealed in 1981 together with the provision for reduced sentences for murder where the motive was protection or restoration of the murderer's or his/her family's honour (i.e. for the murder of a spouse, sister or daughter deemed to be involved in an illegitimate sexual relationship, and/or murder of the other party in that relationship).

17 Tamar Pitch (1990) discusses that process, and the different positions and proposals of political parties and of groups within the feminist movement.

18 For example, the 2007 report noted that survey data indicated 91.6 per cent of rapes were not reported to police (ISTAT 2007: 2).

The six makers of the documentary *A Trial for Rape* were all active in the Collettivo femminista cinema di Roma (Rome Feminist Cinema Collective) and Loredana Rotondo worked for RAI2. The trial concerned was of particular interest to film because of an important parallel with the Circeo trial: Giorgio Zeppieri was one of the defence barristers in both cases,[19] while Tina Lagostena Bassi, who had been present at the Circeo trial, acted for Fiorella.

The presence of a barrister representing the victim/survivor in a rape case warrants explanation for readers unfamiliar with the Italian judicial system, which belongs to the civil-law tradition. In Italy an aggrieved party can be constituted as '*parte civile*' in criminal proceedings, without having to take a separate civil action for damages.[20] The *parte civile* can be represented in court by a barrister, whose role is independent of that of the prosecutor acting for the State.[21] The barrister representing a *parte civile* can examine witnesses and defendants, engage in plea bargaining and negotiation of damages, and, most significantly, deliver speeches on behalf of the aggrieved party to make a case and rebut the defence submissions (Loiacono 2014: 16). In the playscript we refer to Fiorella as 'complainant', and we acknowledge that this is only an approximation of *parte civile*.

An interesting development in Italian judicial practice that was gaining momentum at the time of the documentary was that of allowing an organization or institution to be constituted as additional *parte civile* – co-complainant – in a criminal trial, representing collective interests perceived to be damaged by the crime. Feminist groups began making such applications in relation to rape trials in March 1977 (Lagostena Bassi 1993). In *A Trial for Rape* we hear of two organizations, the Feminist Movement of Latina and the Women's Liberation Movement of Rome, applying unsuccessfully to appear as co-complainants with Fiorella. However, there was nothing stopping the feminists from attending the trial in large numbers.

There are other features of the trial procedure evident in the documentary and play that differ from those typical of anglophone countries belonging to the common-law tradition.[22] There is no jury; rulings are made by a panel of three judges chaired by the

---

19 We refer to the legal representatives as 'barristers' although, as explained by Loiacono (2014: 15), the Italian term '*avvocato*' does not correspond exactly to 'barrister'. The distinction that applies in Australia, for example, between a barrister (representative in court) and a solicitor (intermediary between client and barrister) does not exist in Italy, where an *avvocato* performs the functions of both.

20 Loiacono (2014) writes of the difficulties in translating the term '*parte civile*' into English, since the concept of *parte civile* does not exist in the common-law systems of most anglophone countries. He defines *parte civile* as follows: 'aggrieved party acting in a criminal proceeding to recover damages. The Italian legal system provides for parties who have suffered damage as a result of criminal acts to take action in criminal proceedings, rather than commence a separate civil action' (16).

21 We also refer to the Pubblico Ministero (PM) as the prosecutor, although Loiacono (2014) explains that the PM (literally 'public ministry') is actually the set of public offices that represents the State in criminal proceedings, and recommends the term 'Prosecution' in translation.

22 We assume readers to be familiar in broad terms with legal and judicial procedures in countries belonging to the common-law tradition – such as the UK (except Scotland), Australia, New Zealand, Canada and the USA – which is significantly different from the civil-law system of Italy (and those of most other countries of continental western Europe) (Loiacono 2014), and especially from the form it had in 1978, before significant changes in the Code of Criminal Procedure were enacted in 1989 (Bromley 1992).

presiding judge. Questions are put to the defendants and witnesses only by the judges (usually the presiding judge), including the questions raised by the barristers. Proceedings also allow for a '*confronto*' (discussion), which entails the simultaneous questioning of two people – each of whom may be a witness, defendant or *parte civile* – whose accounts of any important facts or circumstances given under questioning differ; the presiding judge invites them to confirm their statements and/or contest each other's declarations (Bromley 1992: 141). In *A Trial for Rape*, we see Fiorella and one of the Defendants in a *confronto*.

This context of the trial is highly significant: the court in which a barrister is present to act for the complainant provides the forum for the now famous speech by Tina Lagostena Bassi who, in representing Fiorella, delivers a veritable feminist manifesto on rape, patriarchy and rape trials, on behalf, as she says, of all women. The defence barristers' speeches, on the other hand, suggest a possible reason for the mysterious silence from RAI2 on the documentary, despite renewed calls for a re-screening to mark its fortieth anniversary.[23] Journalist Gian Antonio Stella (2019) surmises that the surviving barristers and the relatives of the deceased ones may be 'very belatedly embarrassed by their invasive, titillating examinations, voyeuristic allusions, and boorishly macho speeches' and so may have requested that the documentary not be broadcast again.

Translation of the play *A Trial for Rape* presented major challenges, in addition to those related to legal terminology – notably that of doing justice to the eloquence of the barristers, and that of avoiding the temptation to render the language of the dialogues more contemporary. The process also prompted us to a particular type of examination of the language of the trial that we had not initially anticipated. In light of scholarship by Linda Coates and colleagues (e.g. Coates, Bavelas and Gibson 1994) and Susan Ehrlich (2007) analysing the discourse of rape trials in English-speaking countries, and in particular the ideological work of words used to recount violence, we paid particular attention in the translation to the choice of words for the defendants' acts. We were not only concerned that the translation should closely reflect the discursive effect of the original utterances but became interested in investigating the linguistic devices used.[24] Not surprisingly, we observed that, beyond the obvious element of Zeppieri's blatant reconstruction of the acts as pleasurable, the language of the male characters – Judge, Zeppieri and the Defendants – is characterized throughout by the use of mutualizing terms that put the violent acts into a framework of sexual activity rather than one of assault, denying their unilateral nature.

In contrast, Fiorella's testimony and Tina Lagostena Bassi's speeches consistently reflect a clear distinction between rape and sexual activity; both women were evidently able to fit words to deeds in a way that resisted the prevailing patriarchal discourse. For example, during the questioning, the Judge and Defendants often use the word '*rapporti*' (relations) or the expression '*rapporti carnali*' (sexual relations) – which we chose to translate as 'intercourse' or 'sexual relations', because these are terms to describe sex

---

23 Sara Filippelli (2011) reports that the documentary is available for borrowing from RAI archives for community screenings but is redacted.

24 These will be discussed in a separate forthcoming study by Claire Kennedy and Luciana d'Arcangeli.

in formal language, and both imply interaction, a joint, consensual activity, as does '*rapporti*'. Yet Fiorella and Tina Lagostena Bassi consistently manage to avoid using those words, or any others that suggest a joint act. Furthermore, when Tina Lagostena Bassi says: 'E io non sono il difensore della donna Fiorella, io sono l'accusatore di un certo modo di fare processi per violenza', she uses '*violenza*' not '*violenza carnale*', to describe the type of trial; that is, just 'trial for violence', without any adjective corresponding to 'sexual'. We interpret this as intentional, and have translated that sentence as 'I am not here to defend this woman Fiorella. I am here to accuse. To denounce this manner of conducting rape trials.' We hope the translation conveys our interpretation that, for Tina Lagostena Bassi and Fiorella (and the feminists present in court, and others then and since), rape is not only often accompanied by violence, it *is* violence.

The interviews

We envisioned the interviewing process as a way to obtain insights of practical use to readers who are approaching the writing and staging of plays that highlight, respond to or resist gendered violence. Our interviewees – writers, directors and producers, who span an age range exceeding five decades and have diverse career and activism experiences – are all passionate about theatre as a force for addressing themes of power and inequality. We expected that hearing about a play from the creatives involved would enrich our understanding of their motives and intentions: what ideas, values and challenges might be shared between, or peculiar to, these individual women and men of different generations, now based in Italy, the UK, Australia and Spain?

What emerged from the interviews not only provided information on how each of the plays was created and staged, but also encompassed a number of issues that our interviewees faced as they wrote about and staged VAWG – issues of voice, representation, trauma and reception. As Willis (2021: 23) asks: 'Who may tell the story of another? Who is included and excluded from the act of storytelling? If victims are represented, what are their rights in relation to their own representation? To what extent is it possible for the actor or writer to fully understand the nature of the traumatic violent experience that they are attempting to represent?'

Matters of voice and representation are particularly relevant for the creators of *Little Stitches* and 'Kubra', as none of them comes from a country or diaspora community where FGM/C has been practised as a tradition. They had felt concern from the outset at their lack of knowledge and experience, and the risk of, as Karis Halsall put it, 'preaching about the cultural practices of other communities'. In the interviews, they reported having been encouraged by survivors of FGM/C to proceed, as well as advised and informed. The urgent need for action and education expressed by the survivors they met in their research had assuaged their misgivings. It is clear from their interviews that feelings of uncertainty and inadequacy had arisen for the *Little Stitches* team in relation to matters such as approaching survivors to seek their testimony, concern to avoid letting their own point of view or that of the dominant culture prevail over the survivors' voices, taking decisions regarding race and ethnicity in casting, and choosing images for publicity material. Meanwhile, Maraini's conviction of the rightness of taking a stand on FGM/C was linked to her experience at the Fourth World Conference on Women, a major international conference on women's rights held in 1995 in Beijing, which produced the Beijing Declaration and the Platform for Action (UN WOMEN 2015). Issues of voice and representation also came up in the interview with Chiocca, when we asked about his stance with respect to his adaptation of the 1978 documentary – a man using a work by women filmmakers, a work highlighting the dual violation of a survivor of rape who dares to pursue her attackers in court. Chiocca explained that he approached the work '[not] as a "male author", but as a human being', for whom violence against women is violation of human rights.

Other insights that emerge from the interviews concern possible effects on a cast and crew, and on audience members, of the representation of VAWG. What can be the implications of casting choices? In what ways are actors likely to be seen by audiences as representing particular ethnic groups or other 'categories' of people? These are questions that, as Ainsley Burdell and Nicolette Kay make clear, relate to both the audiences' interpretations and the actors' well-being in their jobs. Then too, how do actors cope with acting out violence, and what happens if they find parts of the dialogue or action too gruelling, too graphic? How can they best be supported? And do we risk abuse of audience members when we subject them to certain material about violence? Kay describes the situation of being told that schools were no longer booking *Hurried Steps* performances because they felt they lacked resources to deal with the effects – in the short term or long term – of their students being triggered to make disclosures of personal experiences as a result of watching the play, and needing specialized support.

The creators of these plays, as is clear from their interviews, are all concerned to achieve a representation of VAWG that is aimed at stimulating positive and urgently needed social change, yet is not sensationalist. Although different insights emerged from the interviews regarding performance spaces, relationships between actors and spectators, staging strategies, lighting, costumes and all things theatrical, all our authors had the following questions in mind: In what ways, if any, can theatre advance a cause for change? How does the staging of violence against women and girls help in challenging our current culture with its endless instances of rape, femicide, child marriage, abuse, FGM/C, trafficking?

The *Little Stitches* team we interviewed spoke of their purpose as raising awareness and stimulating discussion, by providing a forum for survivors' voices and communicating on an emotional level with audiences who were unaware of, or only vaguely informed of, the significance and prevalence of FGM/C. 'Our goal was to keep people talking about this issue, in the hope that that would then contribute towards producing real change', wrote Bahar Brunton. They were encouraged by the response of some spectators, especially survivors, after performances, who thanked them for having brought the issues out for public discussion (as was Olivia Brown by similar responses to 'Kubra' in Sydney). No matter the size of the venue – theatre or library – the team members felt it had been a profound learning experience for all involved, cast, crew and audiences. So the director, Alex Crampton, concluded that the play had made a difference: 'In that small, microcosmic way, you know, even if it was only a few hundred, a thousand people, the situation is better than it was before.'

In her interview, Kay refers to the critical reaction of a panel member in the post-show discussion at a Sydney performance of *Hurried Steps* in 2016. That panel member was Eva Cox, a veteran feminist and social justice campaigner. She expressed concern that, whatever the intentions, plays such as *Hurried Steps* can appear to place the emphasis on women as victims, and that the depiction of women as victims does not encourage action. During the panel discussion she raised the question: 'Does this contribute to a "What we can do about it?" discourse, or does it actually reinforce the idea that the problem is insoluble?' In conversation with us, Cox (2020) explained that the development she would like to see in theatre about VAWG would be oriented towards understanding the causes and working to change the situation – and a shift of focus onto the perpetrators: 'The central question should be about male violence, not violence against women. We need to address men's socialization against women and the construction of masculinity. Why do we raise men to be violent? Why are men's roles defined by their ability to assert themselves physically?'

These kinds of questions illustrate the importance of the discussion sessions following performances of *Little Stitches* and *Hurried Steps*, and those Chiocca held with school students prior to their watching *A Trial for Rape*. The topics discussed when *Hurried Steps* was performed in Australia and New Zealand in 2018 and 2019 (directed by Burdell) included, for example: the implications of a lack of affordable accommodation for women leaving violent situations; access to confidential, free, day-surgery services for de-infibulation in public hospitals; the lack of protection and services for non-citizens subject to violent partners; the over-representation of domestic violence survivors in prisons; the variety of education programmes being conducted by different organizations, including by men for men; and the personal stories of survivors of abuse who have become leaders of campaigns, services, educational programmes and support groups. At these events there were also experienced women on hand specifically for audience members to speak to if they became distressed or felt the need to disclose personal experience individually. It is impossible to attend these events without being struck by the energy and expertise of the panel members – campaigners, educators and providers of support services of various kinds – and the range of work they are doing towards prevention.

The post-show discussions also informed our interviewees, whose reflections drew not only on their experience of creating the works but also observing first-hand the audience responses. And putting this book together has enriched our own understanding and emotional response to the plays, as we hope the book will do for readers.

Finally, a conviction shared by everyone contributing to this book concerns the power of words in theatre and the power of theatre in giving life to words. A firm belief in the importance of theatre as a medium to raise awareness and promote change is reiterated throughout the interviews. Maraini's closing words compare live theatre to drama on screens big and small, and underline the compelling effect of the spoken word and the physical presence of the actor in theatre: 'Take *Hurried Steps*, for example: no sets, no nothing – the power lies in the words. . . . [T]he presence of the physical body of the actor and the power of the spoken word will prevail. Words speak to the mind, and the mind, in the end, is what raises our consciousness.' Chiocca, similarly, speaks of the power he felt in the words of the documentary *A Trial for Rape* and his reaction of wanting to bring those words to life in a different way by means of theatre, as 'theatre forces you to inhabit the same space as the actors, and to hear words spoken live, in a physically shared space and time'.

In closing . . .

Violence against women and girls is a deeply ingrained societal phenomenon based on inequality, whose symptoms are most often manifest in intimate and domestic spheres. Progress towards its elimination has been evident in many parts of the world in recent years, yet new concerns continue to arise. The potential for enabling such violence that is provided by new technological tools, and the worsening of statistics during the Covid-19 pandemic, for example, are cause for alarm. Reforms in law and in procedures of policing and medical responses, while essential, can only be a part of the solution to this complex problem; as has been clearly argued for some time now (for example, Breger 2014; Re 2017: 181), what is also needed is change in cultural norms and social models of behaviour. The arts have a fundamental role in challenging and disrupting these.

Within the arts, theatre holds a special place due to the synchronous relationship that is created during a performance between actors and spectators, as Chiocca and Maraini highlight. The experience of the 'other' – in terms of class, age, gender, ethnicity, nationality, religion, culture and so on – as expressed on stage by the actors, can be felt vicariously by the spectator who shares the same physical space. And this can work to cancel out the distance, both real and metaphorical (whether historical, geographical, or in terms of class, age, etc.), that separates that spectator from the characters on stage – in their uniqueness and at the same time the universality that theatrical characters have always striven for. The plays we have gathered together in this book may bridge the gap to unfamiliar realities, or open up the possibility of recognizing one's own story in that of others.

We leave our readers in the hope that the statistics of VAWG will take on an individual human dimension for them as they have for us, through the stories of Dunya, Felicity, Safa, Kubra, Fiorella, and the unnamed girls and women in these plays. Certainly, the words of the authors, producers and directors who talked and corresponded with us have not only given valuable insight into the aesthetics and ethics of their works, but inspired us even more by their conviction of the power of theatre as a medium to raise awareness and promote change. Indeed, we hope these plays will be read, studied and performed, and that our readers will accept our invitation to delve deeper into the issues and to act to eliminate violence against women and girls.

Luciana d'Arcangeli, Claire Kennedy and Daniela Cavallaro

Little Stitches

Isley Lynn, Raúl Quirós Molina, Bahar Brunton and Karis E. Halsall

Little Stitches premiered at Theatre503 in London on 21 August 2014. In the same season, it was also staged at the Arcola Tent and the Gate Theatre in London.

Cast for *Sleight of Hand*

Daphne Alexander	**Flight Attendant**
Chin Nyenwe	**Ice Cream Van Driver**
Shalini Peiris	**Teacher**
Shuna Snow	**Street Cleaner**
Stephanie Yamson	**Postal Worker**

Cast for *Where Do I Start?*

Daphne Alexander	**Woman**
Chin Nyenwe	**Man**
Shuna Snow	**Nurse**
Stephanie Yamson	**Felicity**

Cast for *Dancing Feet*

Chin Nyenwe	**Man**
Shalini Peiris	**Girl**
Shuna Snow	**Woman 1**
Stephanie Yamson	**Woman 2**

Cast for *Mutant*

Chin Nyenwe	**Dr Chaudhry**
Shalini Peiris	**Safa**
Shuna Snow	**Mother**

Director	Alex Crampton
Assistant Director	Emma Deegan
Producer	Melissa Dean
Co-Producer	Raúl Quirós Molina
Designer	Anna Privitera
Sound Designer	Erik Medeiros
Costume Designer	Fiona Lockton
Lighting Designer	Anna Sbokou

Movement Director	Danny Scott
Stage Manager	Martha Everett
Production	BAREtruth Theatre Company

Little Stitches was performed again on 13 and 14 April 2015, at the Omnibus Theatre in London. The cast members were Nadi Kemp-Sayfi, Jude Owusu, Shuna Snow, Stephanie Yamson and Taniel Yusef.

Sleight of Hand

Isley Lynn

Dedicated to the people of Finsbury Park Road and the girls of the world

Special thanks to: Philipp Ehmann, Romanus Chukwu Emeka-Alum, Roshni Goyate, Sophie Morris, Emily Palmer, Dave Rogers, Hollie Rogers, Adelle Potter, Danielle Wilson

Characters

Teacher, *any gender, any ethnicity, any age, tired smile*
Postal Worker, *any gender, any ethnicity, an immigrant who speaks English with a foreign accent, just about any age, excitable, actor must be able to learn very basic magic tricks and phrases in other languages*
Flight Attendant, *any gender, any ethnicity, British accent, any age, hardened, tells it like it is*
Ice Cream Van Driver, *male, any ethnicity, British accent, youngish, alternatively dressed*
Street Cleaner, *any gender, any ethnicity, any age, direct*

Notes

Any text in square brackets – [ ] – is unspoken and included only to clarify the meaning of the rest of the line.

Line divisions are placed to indicate a change or slight shift in thought and do not necessarily indicate pauses or beats.

At no point do the characters ever acknowledge each other on stage.

Postal Worker, Teacher, Flight Attendant and Ice Cream Van Driver all address the audience:

Teacher
Their last task for the day is to draw a picture of what they're going to do on their summer holidays

Postal Worker
I wanted to be a magician when I was little

Flight Attendant
I bet I'll be a lifer
Which frankly is depressing

Teacher
We've put the two Year 3 classes together and they're spread out across the floor with their paper and pencils
They're mostly doing a very good job of sharing

Ice Cream Van Driver
It was a fucking retarded idea
I know that
Not retar – sorry, not –

Postal Worker
Did a lot of it at school
In the playground, you know

Ice Cream Van Driver
Fucking nutting bonkers, I mean
Definitely not a sound business decision

Teacher
And we just watch

Postal Worker
Card tricks, sleight of hand
That sort of thing

Ice Cream Van Driver
But I don't regret it
No way

Teacher
Dunya is a very sweet girl
Very very sweet, very popular
And she was very upset when she found out she needed glasses this year
So her mother let her pick whatever ones she wanted
Bright pink, almost neon pink rims, thick and round, with butterflies cut into the side
She loves wearing them
Smart mum
She's drawing herself and some other people surrounded by presents with big bows

1 From left: Shalini Peiris (Teacher), Chin Nyenwe (Ice Cream Van Driver), Daphne Alexander (Flight Attendant) and Stephanie Yamson (Postal Worker) in *Sleight of Hand*. Theatre503, London, 21 August 2014. Photo courtesy of John Wilson.

A celebration
A birthday party
And there are lots of planes in the sky

Flight Attendant
There's three types of cabin crew
Lifers are the worst
They're the stereotypes
Flamboyantly gay guys, bitchy girls
Middle-aged sad cases in a permanent mid-life crisis
Uniforms bulging at the waist
Maybe a button hanging off
Lipstick on their teeth
Then there's the ones that treat it as like a gap year
Thinking they'll do it for a bit and leave and that's that
Then there's the people like me who do it cos they think they could actually really make something of it and it ends up really –
Really screwing them up
Honestly

Teacher
Next to her is Jeethi
She – this is incredible actually – her cousin escaped a forced marriage

They were taking her back to India
Apparently when she found out what was going to happen
And this was only very late
She put a spoon
In her underwear
So when the metal detectors went off they had to take her aside to search her and
that's when she said she needed help
Can you believe that!
So clever
Almost took up a whole lesson, talking about that
The rest of Show and Tell completely abandoned
We talked about arranged marriages
What was good and bad about them, why they happen
And Dunya asked question after question, couldn't get enough
They've been friends ever since
Jeethi is drawing sea creatures

Flight Attendant
This mum and daughter in the bulkhead right by my seat must be petrified of flying
They're so quiet
Holding hands

Postal Worker
If I catch the children on their way to school I'll treat them to a penny from their ear
or something
Postal Worker makes a coin appear in the air, then throws it up and catches it.
Or sometimes if I meet someone as they're coming out of the house I'll take one of
the rubber bands from around their post and put it on my two fingers like this –
*Postal Worker has fished out a rubber band, from their pocket perhaps, and
demonstrates the trick as they describe it:*
– and just click my fingers and – it jumps!

Teacher
Nadia is in tears
Has been all day
Her face is blotched and red and she's refusing to use the coloured pencils
She's moving house
So this really is the last day for her
And being with all her friends
She's drawing lots and lots of very sad faces

Postal Worker
Again I just click my fingers and – it jumps back!
Postal Worker laughs.
It's what I'm known for now
And I know just about everyone on my routes
Their names and everything
Just about

Teacher
It's taken me half a year but I can tell the twins apart now
Which they like to test by lying and saying I've got it wrong
Danielle is better at lying than Petra so then I always know for sure
Petra is drawing a football game and Danielle is drawing what I think must be Disneyland
They're on opposite sides of the room

Postal Worker
Sometimes if I see someone off somewhere I'll just get their post and hold it out to them
Postal Worker holds out some post, smug and nonchalant.
The look on their faces!
Postal Worker laughs.
'How did you know . . .?'
Postal Worker laughs.
You can hear the cogs turning, the fuses blowing in their brains
Postal Worker laughs.
That's what it's all about for me
A little bit of wonder in their day
So it's not so different I don't think
Beat.
Not strictly allowed to do that
But I'm always right so there's been no problems

Teacher
Sam is always late and her clothes are always dirty and she always falls asleep at about 11.30 and she gets a free meal
A lot of the children do
But she –
They always give her a bit more
She's drawing a long winding road with lots of trees

Ice Cream Van Driver
My results weren't great
Shit for brains
Always knew that
But might have done better if Mum hadn't died
Right over GCSEs
Quite fucking shit
Was going to buy to let with the inheritance
Be a thieving scumbag landlord
Be a player in the housing crisis
That was the plan
But when I see it . . .
And it's literally, actually, literally falling apart

Masking tape holding it up
But fuck me
I fell in love

Teacher
Rebecca calls Hollie fat
And she's not exactly a stick insect herself
She's drawing a crowded swimming pool
Now, Hollie is very overweight
And I don't think it's anything to do with her parents or her diet or exercise
I think she's just fat
Biologically fat
She's drawing herself swimming with dolphins
And Jessica has the beginnings of an eating disorder
Which shocked me at first
But I did some research and apparently it's not that uncommon
People think because they're so young that this stuff doesn't touch them
It touches them
And to me it seems it's getting younger and younger . . .
Jessica
She's drawing a blue, cloudy sky full of hot-air balloons

Ice Cream Van Driver
It was just a bog standard van
Had to get it kitted out, all fitted in by some tubby cunt in Battersea
Twenty K for a pump that does Mr Whippys
Can you fucking believe that?
And yes
First thing I did
Cheeky mouthful straight from the spout
Childhood dream: accomplished
Put my bitching graffiti skills to use and did it up over the bank holiday weekend
Worked my arse off
And it was worth it
I mean
Come on
You've got to admit
It's pretty special
Not special like – you know what I mean
Actually special
You don't see them like this do you

Teacher
I've been really pushing for Monique to get special help but the parents won't have it
I don't know if they're in complete denial about how far behind she is
Or if they know full well and don't want her treated any differently

Which I completely sympathise with
But the truth is I can't do my job
She takes up all my energy, she needs so much help
Anyway she's drawing a house

Flight Attendant
I get asked all the time
It gets boring

Teacher
Selina's parents think she's gifted
She's not gifted
She's spoiled
I feel sorry for her siblings
They're treated so differently, you wouldn't believe
She's drawing a campfire and lots of people around it holding hands

Flight Attendant
'What's the most amazing place you've ever been to'
And I say 'Barbados'
I have a friend who's really into clubbing and she asked me once what the most amazing city
I'd ever been to was
And I'm, like, London
And she laughs at me
And I tell her it's the best city in the whole world because it's all the world's cities in one
Isn't it
And you can't get decent Indian in America, I'm telling you

Teacher
Maria
Who actually is gifted
Is much better behaved
She really is the perfect child
She's my favourite
Not because she's gifted
Because she's easy
She's drawing her pet cat in shocking detail

Flight Attendant
Truth is I don't even know the places I go that well
Because legally you have to spend some time on the ground before you fly home
But you're just too tired to do anything
And you don't know anyone there
So you just watch the Disney channel in your hotel room
You're in a constant state of jet lag so you can't sleep
So you pop a couple of tablets and lose half the time that way

My mum says I really should stop taking them but I'm not fussed honestly
It helps me cope, so
And that's what I can't wait for today because it's just one of those flights you know
The works
And I almost lose it once or twice but I keep my cool because I'm better than that
I'm very good at my job

Teacher
I know 100 per cent that Tiffany is gay
It's not just a tomboy thing
And it is a gene, so . . .
She's drawing a dog which I think is a caterpillar until I'm corrected, which is a pretty common occurrence

Ice Cream Van Driver
At first the biggest challenge was keeping a lid on the language around the kids
Got a handle on it now but it's a fucking effort
First up is the lunch round and either you can go to the city wankers or the Dalston dickheads
Either way it's a killing
Loads of blokes buying 99s for the girls
Some sort of nostalgia thing
Makes them look very cool and alternative and interesting
Well, they fucking aren't
Then you do the after-school runs
Only the ratty estate schools because the yummy mummy gluten-free organic stitch 'n' bitch brigade complain about the E numbers or the sugar or whatever
Then you go round their houses where they all run riot I swear

Teacher
I know 100 per cent that Tyra will end up in prison
I think she knows too, in a way
It's where her mum is
She's drawing a car

Ice Cream Van Driver
Is it just me or are kids so much fucking ruder than we were at their age?
Or do I just think that because I'm a proper adult now?

Teacher
I know 100 per cent that Rhian will be a teenage mother
She cares far too much about what other people think of her
She'll sleep with the first boy who asks
She's drawing a beach

Ice Cream Van Driver
I'm a proper entrepreneur
I'm old
Shit

Teacher
Kayra is Turkish and when she got here she couldn't speak any English
And I think she's older than her parents say she is
And she's honestly a bit of a mystery
And she kicks
And bites
And she speaks well now but sometimes when she's angry or frustrated she'll just express herself physically
She's punching holes in the paper with a pencil
It's the end of the year
Let her punch holes in the paper

Flight Attendant
I get paid more than most
Because I go for the difficult flights
They pay differently depending on the country and it's only a little to do with how far away it is
Really, secretly, it's the nationalities

Postal Worker
I know a lot of languages too
A little from a lot of languages
Bits and pieces
Everyone here does
Walk down Blackstock and you won't hear English
I like to be able to say a little something, doesn't really matter what it is, to all the families on my streets

Flight Attendant
We've got this bidding system
Doesn't always work but you're pretty much guaranteed a flight to Africa if you bid for it – which I do
Because nobody likes the Nigerians
That's just a fact

Postal Worker
I speak fluent French but there isn't anyone French on this street
'Je suis désolé, le chien a mangé vos lettres!'
[I'm sorry, the dog has eaten your letters!]
Postal Worker laughs.
No, there's mostly British and Indian
God, their houses
You'd think people were squatting but no it's just the Indians

Flight Attendant
Now don't get me wrong
Brits aren't saints either
They're stuck-up, they're snobs

And Americans are loud and the Japanese are two-faced, all smiles on the flight but they always complain later, behind your back, in writing

Postal Worker
But they're beautiful people you know
They are, I mean that

Flight Attendant
The flight to Nigeria – the route I'm on today – only five and a half hours but nobody wants it because they're shouty and greedy and rude

Postal Worker
'Namaste. Kasa kai? Thik hai'
[Hello. How are you? I'm well]

Flight Attendant
I don't think they're really rude really
It's just their culture isn't it
They don't say please or thank you
They hiss at you
To get your attention
Pull on your gilet too
Actually tug your clothes
It's insane
As you're walking up the aisle
Never stop eating
Massive women
With all this fabric and about five kids hanging off them and running around all the time
It does your head in

Postal Worker
All people are beautiful
You reach out to someone and you'll always find beauty
I promise you
It's hiding in plain sight
Postal Worker laughs.
Some Polish too
'Meisien piwny rosnie, co?'
[I can see your beer muscles are growing bigger]
Postal Worker laughs.
It's so nice to see them brighten up
Think about it
You're in the middle of London
Thousands and thousands and thousands of miles from home
Your real home
And someone calls you a fatty in your own language!
Postal Worker laughs.
Everyday magic!

Flight Attendant
And this family in the bulkhead are definitely African but they're being so still, so quiet, I did wonder
Not complaining!
And I notice
– And this is a bit weird –
They're not holding hands
She's grabbing her wrist
The mum is holding on to the daughter for dear . . . [life]
And they still haven't gotten up or anything or talked at all
She must have a real phobia of flying
I think they're praying
She's muttering under her breath sort of constantly, the mum
And this little phrase she keeps repeating
Mumble mumble Dunya mumble mumble Dunya Dunya mumble mumble
And they both look upset
Flight Attendant sighs.
I hope they're not terrorists
You do get African terrorists
Just not on planes

Teacher
Hannah is as good as gold but always acts up at the end of the day
She's got an older brother who's always getting detention and either she wants to be like her brother and stay behind or she wants to stay behind because she doesn't want to go home
For some reason
I've brought it up with Student Welfare
They're looking into it
Or maybe she just gets tired
But my suspicions are confirmed, I think, because when it's clean-up time she goes berserk and refuses to do anything and pushes Monique and I have to put her in the Thinking Chair
It's worse than usual today because she'll be home for a long time, not just a weekend, you see
She hasn't drawn anything
Just filled the page with colour
Just colour

Ice Cream Van Driver
It's the last school day before the summer holidays
Got some festivals lined up
Gonna be motherfucking badass
Just pitch up, listen to some music, do your thing, go back to your tent
Sweet
On the streets here you can't stay anywhere more than fifteen minutes without moving on

Pain in the bollocks
It's the law though
And some places are alright but other neighbourhoods are really on it
And when I see this one twat coming down the street I know he's not going to let me off lightly, he never fucking does
Dog-nosed little Nazi
So I close up and disappoint all the kids who've been waiting patiently and I always point to that bobby coming down so they know exactly what the police force is really responsible for
Ice Cream Van Driver holds his fist up.
And I put on the little tune
Ice Cream Van Driver whistles part of the tune his ice-cream van plays.
Gets on your tits after a while but really it's the best part of the job
And as I round the corner I see these two little girls sort of pressed up against the bush away from all the other kids
Like they were out for me but changed their minds
And it's a funny image because they're all covered up with head scarves and everything
But one of them's got these bright pink frankly wicked glasses on
And the other one's got their skirt out like this
Ice Cream Van Driver mimes holding out the waistband of a skirt.
And the speccy one's peering down like she's looking into a fucking well or something
Like she's going to fall in
And I slow down
And smile
Not like! Not like, nothing like that
Fucking –
No!

Postal Worker
That house is empty
Still not sold
Siblings fighting over their cut I suspect

Ice Cream Van Driver
Just we used to do that
Showing each other what we had down there
On school trips at the back of the bus when the sweets were going round so no one paid us any attention
And I remember being really . . .
Like there was so much in the world to find out
And I had it all ahead of me
I had a cracking childhood
Mum made sure of that
I miss it

I miss her
And I miss being at the back of the school bus
And being a carefree innocent little kid and completely –
And being really fucking happy
That's all
Anyway . . .
Um
Beat.
The speccy girl looks like she's just had the shock of her life
Like she's never seen another fanny before!

Postal Worker
I found her
Oh yeah
Noticed a funny smell through the slot
Turned out she was right the other side of the door!
Yeah
Post piling up
If it's a family house you're alright, they're just away somewhere
But if it's a pensioner
Postal Worker shakes their head.
So I can play a very important role in the community
If something's out of place
I'm the one who knows about it

Ice Cream Van Driver
She's dar– *[dark]*, bla– *[black]*, um, brown skinned you know, yeah
But it's like there's no colour in her face whatsoever
It is quite hilarious actually
She's dropped this big drawing in surprise
Ice Cream Van Driver giggles.
It sort of surfs over to the van
You know the way paper does
It's very colourful
It's like a party scene
Loads of presents
Planes, too, for some fucking reason
It's pretty good
My drawings were all shit at that age
This is –
It's bloody brilliant actually

Teacher
Bethany is fine
Nothing special
But she's probably the happiest girl in the class

And she'll probably continue to be as an adult
It's a real achievement to be ordinary, actually
There are so many other things that you could be
That all the other children are
It's very hard to keep track
She's drawing herself riding a horse

Postal Worker
Yeah I keep an eye on everyone
It's like a little patrol

Flight Attendant
Zenelle was on a flight once where there was this mum with her baby
Didn't move the whole time
And the mum didn't feed it or even look down at it and just stared at the seat in front of her
So Zenelle told the pilot who told the airport they were flying into and when they landed they found out the baby was dead
And
Filled with drugs
It's true
I shit you not
After that they offered us all training in spotting things like that
Human trafficking, that sort of thing
But you know what
I've got my own problems
Let someone else lose sleep over it
Zenelle's really into it now

Postal Worker
So when I hear what I'm hearing I'm on alert
Probably just some boys scuffling
But through the little B&Q fence they've put up
I see two bodies wrestling around
And there's a woman shouting
So I speed up my walking
Get past the fence to see it's a woman
And a little girl
Must be her little girl
I know her!
Um . . .
Postal Worker clicks their fingers, trying to remember.
Dunya
That's it
Do you know what a lepidopterist is?
Neither did I
But Dunya does!

A butterfly scientist!
What a girl!
I always greet her like this –
Postal Worker makes glasses with their upturned hands.
'Hello Partner!'
Postal Worker laughs.
She loves it!
. . .
Wow, she's really getting a telling-off
And Dunya's readjusting her clothes
And the car in their driveway is stuffed to the brim with suitcases
I've never seen so many

Teacher
And at the end of the day Dunya runs past me with her picture in her hands, all proud
Shows me the aeroplanes, the presents, I tell her it's wonderful

Postal Worker
And she's waving something in her hands
Which she throws away in a fit of, I don't know
God she is angry
And it lands by my feet
A little metal spoon

As Ice Cream Van Driver speaks, Postal Worker bends down and 'picks up' a spoon (actually they produce it themselves) and holds it up to inspect it –

Ice Cream Van Driver
Ohp
They've noticed me now
I think the van's completely stopped now
I feel like a pervert just looking at them

Postal Worker
They've noticed me now
The mother's quiet

Flight Attendant
And every so often I catch that girl's eyes
Through those ridiculous specs
I mean what was her mum thinking
Bloody butterflies
I know she's little but they're just tacky
Won't stop staring at me
Needs teaching some manners

Postal Worker
(*referring to the spoon*)   There's nothing special about it
Silence

Looking at me
Postal Worker makes sure they have everyone's attention, then makes the spoon
disappear.
It's my favourite trick
Normally I do it with a pen
But it doesn't matter what
Just something small but significant
Changes
Disappears
And it was right in front of you
And now it's gone
And you didn't even see it happen
And I could do it again and again and you'd never see it
Right in front of your eyes and you never see it
Incredible
Beat.
Postal Worker laughs.
And the mum laughs back
Awkwardly
I hold out the now-magic spoon to the little girl
Whose eyes are so wide
But not like they should be
Not full of wonder
Full of . . .

Teacher
(*only realizing halfway through that they don't know her actual birthday*)   'Oh,
Dunya! Happy birthday for um – in a – (*pointing at her picture*) – you know in a – in
a little while'
She gives me a funny look
And runs out
And as she turns to dash out the door, the light catches her glasses and they flash back
at me
Like a magic trick

Flight Attendant
And I've just finished landing prep and I sit in my seat and have to look them all in
the face as we descend
The one with the screaming twins

Postal Worker
The mother takes the spoon
Silly woman

Flight Attendant
The one that spilled their own rum and diet coke and wanted a free one

Postal Worker
The child always gets the magical object

Ice Cream Van Driver
'Do you want a free flake?'
Is that just even more pervy?
And they just shake their heads

Flight Attendant
And that little girl in the glasses has been really really quiet the whole time
And I can't ignore it

Ice Cream Van Driver
And there is definitely something wrong
Because who turns down a free flake?

Postal Worker
'Ebe Ka Ina Eje'
I say
Where are you going in Ibo – they're African
She answers in English
Postal Worker shrugs.
They're going on holiday
Back home

Flight Attendant
And now she's looking out the window as the bright green African ground gets closer
and little tears are wetting the pink plastic frames, are rolling down her . . .
A sudden lump in Flight Attendant's throat, which surprises them.
They compose themselves.

Postal Worker
Lovely
'Have a nice trip'

Teacher
I just think
And I feel terrible, but
I can just forget about them
The whole term you're watching them so intently
Not just in lessons but generally
Trying to catch any little clue something might need your attention
Because you want them to be happy
Successful
All of that
You're raising them, really
For some of them they spend more time with you than they do with their parents
But in the holidays
The long holidays

You can't do anything
You don't have to care
And you feel sane again

Flight Attendant
I don't know why it sets me off
I don't know why she's crying

Ice Cream Van Driver
(*shrugs*)   Their loss
So I drive on

Flight Attendant
Probably didn't get the teddy she wanted

Ice Cream Van Driver
Probably can't have any
Probably something to do with their religion
Fucking stupid
You gotta let kids be kids don't you

Flight Attendant
(*uncomfortable*)   I wish she'd get a grip
I mean for god's sake

Ice Cream Van Driver whistles the tune his ice-cream van plays underneath:

Flight Attendant
And I don't care who sees me I get a tablet out of my pocket and swallow it without
water because I don't want to even wait a second when I get to the hotel, I want to be
out of it ASAP, I just want to get off this plane, get away from this girl, get to my
hotel room, get into bed, get to sleep and get back
And do it all again

Ice Cream Van Driver
[I] Fucking love my job

Teacher
And I realize
It's not her birthday
Her birthday was in February
She brought in fairy cakes
. . . Huh

Flight Attendant
And I look out the window

Postal Worker
Hello, Missus . . . yes fine, you . . .

*As they all say their speeches over the top of one another, Street Cleaner approaches
from the back or side of the stage and walks right to the front and centre.*

Postal Worker

. . . I'm afraid not, next week . . . Alright you take care . . . Bye-bye . . . Hey ciao, bella! *[Hi, beautiful!]* (*Postal Worker laughs.*) Come stai? . . . Bene, bene! *[How are you? . . . Well, well]* Hey – Parallelepipedo! *[Parallelogram]* (*Postal Worker laughs.*) . . . Ciao, ciao . . . Namaste . . . Morning sir . . . *etc.*

Ice Cream Van Driver

Hello . . . Coming up . . . No problem . . . There you are . . . Thanks . . . Hold on I just need another 20p . . . Brilliant, thank you . . . You too . . . Uh I think she was next little man . . . Yes I think so . . . Sure thing . . . And chocolate? . . . And gummies? . . . If you say so . . . *etc.*

Teacher

Bye-bye . . . You too . . . Sam – Samantha! . . . Tuck your shirt in please . . . Thank you . . . Bye-bye . . . Blazer Selina . . . I know it's hot . . . You are still a student of this school even if it is the holidays . . . Goodbye . . . OK goodbye . . . Bye-bye Hollie . . . Thank you Monique, you have a good holiday too . . . *etc.*

Flight Attendant

Goodbye sir . . . Thank you . . . Thank you . . . Have a nice day . . . Thank you, have a nice day . . . Thank you . . . Goodbye . . . Goodbye . . . Goodbye, have a nice day . . . Thank you for flying with us . . . Thank you, goodbye . . . Goodbye . . . *etc.*

They stop speaking. Only Street Cleaner is left in light.

Street Cleaner

I have seen people
Looking for a bin
See me
And drop it
On the floor
Their bottle or chicken box or what have you
And give me a nod
Like they're doing me a favour
I have my friendlies
People who smile
Make a real effort
Get their little ones to say hello too
One even knows my name
But mostly people try not to look
Not make direct eye contact
They'd be embarrassed to be doing this
So they think I must be
I'm not
Must think I've been in prison or something
And if I was what of it?
It's a good job
It suits me
It's not as bad as you think

Mornings after match nights are the worst
Broken glass
Takeaway boxes
Vomit
I don't touch that
And I feel sorry for the bin men
Got to be so fit to do that job
Hulking those bags around
And no proper bins for them
Like from the council
All these old Victorian houses they got like bin cupboards
People just bung their stuff in them
So when the bin men come they don't always get it all
I don't blame them
Amalgamate your shit people
It's not hard
Give them a hand
And when it's windy it blows about sometimes
So on bin day it can even be worse, not better
Stuff everywhere
If it's their side of the wall outside their house it's their own problem
Out in the street and it's my business
So when I see it . . .

. . .

And technically it's the other side of the wall to me
So I should just ignore it

. . .

But I can't
Can I

. . .

I could smell it before I saw it actually
It was sour
Wafting on the breeze
Disgusting
People are animals, I thought
But then I saw the . . .
Source
A dress
A small dress
Covered in

Butterflies
Long sleeves
A kiddy's dress
Bottom half
Smothered in
Bad blood
Poking out of the scattered pile of rubbish
Just underneath the living-room window
The other side of the wall

. . .

What could have . . .?

. . .

Not my job

. . .

What would I do with it anyway?
The police?

. . .

Not my responsibility

. . .

Street Cleaner stares.
Street Cleaner looks around.
Street Cleaner reaches out.
Street Cleaner brings their hand up and out in front of them.
And it's thick and stiff with it
But I'm surprised
Because it's so light
In my hand

Where Do I Start?

Raúl Quirós Molina

This play is written using real testimonies of people we interviewed during our research process on FGM in the UK. However, this play doesn't represent any particular individual's opinions, and the stories have been modified and mixed to serve the purpose of staging.

Characters

Nurse
Woman, *Spanish*
Man
Felicity, *thirties, Black*

Notes

– means the character is interrupted by something or someone.
. . . means the character's voice trails off.

Nurse If you want to write a play about FGM, you must see pictures of what type III looks like in reality –

Woman I think what you're doing is great, but you're going to need a real survivor in your play, someone who really understands what it is like going through FGM. Otherwise, how are you going to prove your point? –

Man FGM is particularly problematic because it has been hijacked by a certain kind of radical feminism that sees men as perpetrators and women as victims. In fact, it has largely passed Western feminism by, perhaps because it is confined to immigrant communities – and because it's carried out by women.

Nurse If you want to engage with the community, you need an old person speaking out, someone the audience can identify with and respect –

Man Of course everyone is against FGM –

Nurse FGM is everybody's business –

Woman This could be the new *Vagina Monologues* –

Man I've been volunteering and researching for Amnesty International and other charities here in London for several decades – and it has taken all these years and tonnes of petitions just to get the Education Secretary to write to schools about the issue for the first time –

Nurse Anyone, any race can be affected, not only black or brown women –

Woman At the end of the day, you need to address the play to affected communities –

Nurse Do you know where Kurdistan is? You know what Kurdish people look like? They have white skin and green eyes.

Woman How can you get white middle-class people interested in these issues?

Nurse So I make no distinctions, anyone, anyone coming into my clinic could be a survivor –

Felicity My name isn't going to be on this, yeah? Alright. Where do I start? From the moment I was cut?

Pause.

Nurse Some women come to the clinic with problems when having their first experience of sexual intercourse. Some of them have recently got married and they discover on their wedding night they were cut. And they say to me:

Woman 'Oh, it's just a little cut.'

Nurse So I give them a mirror. We are women, there's trust between us, and we are in a private room –

Felicity I realised I had been subject to FGM after a sex education session –

Nurse I tell them, go and have a look at the mirror and tell me if you only have a small cut. Some of these girls have never seen another vagina in their lives –

Felicity   They tell you, discover your body, sit down in front of a mirror, relax, you are becoming a woman, blah blah, but when I take a mirror, I check myself down there, and then I check the picture in the book . . . I see there is something wrong. And I begin to think I'm ill. I try to talk to my mum about it and she immediately shoos me away –

Woman   There are cases like the rich surgeon in Egypt. He was in the operating theatre with his wife, while she was giving birth, and when the baby was out, he said:

Man   'Can you stitch up to here, can you leave it closed up to here?'

Woman   This of course wouldn't happen in the UK –

Felicity   I'm sorry but I think I need a fag.

She exits.

Nurse   It wouldn't happen in the NHS because there are procedures and policies, they are vigilant, and now it's compulsory to report any FGM case – despite what the tabloids have been saying. But who knows what's happening in private clinics? . . . This (*makes the sign of money*) can get you anything, you know?

Woman   You need to tell these people: this is child abuse, this won't be tolerated here. It's not culture, it's not religion, it's child abuse, plain and simple. But there's a lack of willingness. In France, girls from practising communities are routinely checked.

Nurse   I don't like the French approach, and I think it's very dangerous going down that route. What they are going to achieve is to drive the cutters underground. Just look at how badly they managed the hijab issue! –

Man   Look, the way all these people talk about implementing policies . . . Calling it abuse – that's unhelpful. The UN, for instance, is great at banning FGM but they are useless when talking to communities. You just can't say to them –

Woman   'Don't do this' –

Man   Because they'll get scared and close down. What you are doing is referring to these communities in pejorative terms –

Nurse   You don't threaten them, you don't say –

Man   'We're going to take the kids from you!'

Nurse   And that's exactly what happened with the police before. They stormed into houses, took the children away, and charged the parents.

Man   Do you honestly think children subjected to FGM are going to report their parents and risk being taken away by the police? At least in France there have been more than 100 convictions while in the UK we have had none. The practice has already gone underground.

Pause.

Woman   When working on the ground, in Somalia – where it's actually banned – in Sierra Leone, in other countries I've seen there've been huge improvements. But then a war breaks out, all of a sudden they become refugees, they're sent to a different country and the only way to feel attached to your own culture is by reaffirming your traditions – even in a radical way. When I was working in Eritrea, women were saying . . .

Man   'I'm not going to cut my little girl.'

Woman   They will say they have cut their girls to their leaders, but they won't cut them, in the hope that they will never find out. They cheat on their communities to protect their children –

Nurse   It doesn't matter where it's being done. It's about changing the next generation, so they don't do it to their daughters. Here we don't patronise, we don't force anybody to do anything, to say anything. We organise women's health workshops, for the community, and we raise questions such as –

Man   'How often do you feel stress?'

Nurse   'Do you want to quit smoking?'

Woman   'Are you eating properly?'

Man   'Are your kids OK?'

Nurse   'Right, let's talk about sexual matters.' And that is when you bring up the subject of FGM. But you bring it up from the health point of view.

Pause.

Woman   I've been doing this for several years. I always had an interest in health issues. One of my first destinations was Somalia. A guy who had previous experience there told me:

Man   'Don't forget to try a proper Somalian coffee at terminal B in Mogadishu airport, it's just delicious.'

Woman   Well, when I went there, there was no terminal B . . . Nor terminal A. The airport is nothing more than a dusty road in the middle of the desert. The coffee joke, ha-ha. But this can give you an idea of what situations we're working with. An ambulance can take up to two days to arrive at the location where a woman giving birth is bleeding to death. But we use this as a weapon – sorry, as a tool – to explain the problems that can arise due to FGM –

The following could be said with the characters all speaking at once:

Nurse	Woman	Man
Delay in healing, pelvic infection, keloid scarring, fistula, do you know what keloid scarring is?	Emotional, psychological, infertility, problems with labour and delivery . . .	Pain, bleeding, blood poisoning, may contribute to HIV – or hepatitis, because one cut girl can be ill . . .

Woman   And when you explain to them:

Nurse   'This could happen to your wife, or to your daughter.'

Woman   Then they have second thoughts about it. I had my coffee, eventually. I was invited by a community leader, a big honour I couldn't refuse. But did you know they don't put sugar in the coffee? They use salt . . .

Everybody laughs. **Felicity** *comes back. Sudden silence.* **Felicity** *sighs.*

Felicity   I don't interact much with my community in London – I'm not interested. I was asked to talk to kids at schools about the issue, so I went to this Catholic school and they were terrified, they cringed when they saw a vagina in my slides.

Laughs.

Then I went to this other school and there was a teenager there. I could see he was from my country. We recognised each other, you could tell from his facial features what tribe he's from . . . But then . . . He spent the whole workshop watching YouTube videos on his smartphone! And this happens to us all the time. I don't know, he probably thought that by doing that he was being more respectful to his elders, or his traditions.

Man   Let me tell you about my discussion on FGM with the imam and some other men at a South London mosque. One of the men confirmed that FGM isn't mentioned in the Qu'ran and in fact he preaches against it, and he agreed that the Holy Book says that men and women should be treated with equal respect. But when I asked the men why they permitted female circumcision they said it was allowed in their other Holy Book, the Hadith.

Nurse   If you want to take the play to a mosque, good luck! We tried running workshops there, and ye . . . eah they will let you into the mosque, but then nobody will come –

Man   In any case, none of their wives or daughters had been cut.

Woman   But, let's be clear, this is not about Islam, or Christianity, it is about ignorance.

Nurse   If these women could read, if they could lay their hands on a Holy Book they would understand that it's not in there! –

Man   But that's what religion is, isn't it? It's about 'taming' women's sexual impulses. On top of that, as globalisation has expanded, the feeling of 'us' and 'them' has grown, and the female body seems to be the battlefield. We see our women as sexually liberated, empowered; they see Western women as unclean, a source of the degeneration of our decadent society –

Woman   'Whores' to put it bluntly.

Man   My hope is that one day the younger generation of Somalis here, boys and girls, will watch porn and realise what uncut genitals look like.

Nurse   But this problem isn't exclusive to the Muslim world – it's practised in:

Nurse	Woman	Man
Somalia, Egypt, Eritrea, Gambia, Guinea . . .	Bahrain, Iran, Jordan, Kuwait, Oman, Qatar, Yemen, Palestine . . .	Colombia, Pakistan, Afghanistan, India, Turkey . . .

Man   And now it's happening here. Of course it happens. In the UK.

Silence.

Felicity   I have a Scottish boyfriend. Yeah. I've always had a penchant for white tall men. I mean, African men are alright, I have dated some of them, but I've always liked white men. My parents don't know about him, you don't bring people around, it's not like that in our culture. But, yeah, they can sense something is going on. My brothers and sisters know. But nothing can be said at home, not until there's some physical evidence, like a blond baby, (*laughs*) you know what I mean . . .

On top of that, it's quite complicated, because my boyfriend was brought up as a Catholic, and I'm Muslim – not very religious these days though – so if we marry, he's supposed to rot in hell if he doesn't convert to Islam, or I'm supposed to rot in their hell if I don't convert, I don't know, something like that. But this is not about religion, come on. Religion is about getting on together, having a community, acting as a family . . . –

Nurse   You have to be very very tactful when dealing with a case of FGM. Faith, one of the survivors I worked with, referred herself to the clinic. She had just got married, and was having problems with intercourse.

Woman   In type III the vagina can be the size of a finger or a pencil. So what if the husband wants to have sex, and he can't have it . . . It can get very nasty for the woman . . .

Nurse   The GP had no idea what to do, so the girl googled our clinic, and called. She wanted information about having it reversed. I was the one who picked up the call and the first thing she says is:

Man   'I don't want to be contacted by you. I will call you.'

Nurse   She didn't want her family to know and be shamed. (*Pause.*) Eventually she had a de-infibulation, everything was successful and she has referred a friend.

Woman   There's a wave of awareness for FGM every five, ten years. But now, now it's not a wave, it's a tsunami. There hasn't been a prosecution in all these years, and now there's two –

Nurse   And not a day goes by without the *Evening Standard* publishing something about FGM. But it's still not easy. A woman called Hope contacted us to have a de-infibulation, she had been married for a short time, and the usual, she had problems. She was referred by her twin sister, who'd had a reversal procedure two years before!

Man   It took two years for the sister to tell her she'd had a de-infibulation.

Woman   More and more community leaders are speaking out, I mean, we have monthly meetings with people working in our areas . . . I worked in Africa for five-odd years and things have changed radically there . . .

Nurse   Families are changing. While the older sisters have had it done, the little ones no longer do. Once the mothers understand that it's not beneficial, that it's dangerous, they fight against the tradition . . . We are extremely busy in London – not only in boroughs with a high percentage of population at risk, but also in Westminster, Chelsea, . . .

Man   Unfortunately I don't know many survivors, so I can't put you in contact with them – but I'm sure Forward or Amnesty International can.

Felicity   Where do you want me to start? From the minute I was cut? (*Pause.*) I blacked out the experience, to be honest. Sorry. Where should I start, then? We came to the UK fleeing the war. One of my first memories is a road with piles of dead bodies on the side, and being told not to speak, so no one would recognise where we were from, because soldiers could tell from our accent which tribe we belonged to. We arrived at a refugee camp close to the border and the Red Cross flew us here, my uncle had applied for the visa on our behalf.

But before that I was cut in my hometown, along with other relatives and friends. I think it was cheaper that way. They gave us presents, nothing too special, these girly, puffy dresses, because the dress got spoilt with all the blood afterwards.

It was a big day, I remember counting down the days to the event. It's called Gudis. The floor was tiled, I saw same type of floor in Spain, to keep the heat off, very

2 Stephanie Yamson as Felicity in *Where Do I Start?* Omnibus Theatre, London, April 2015. Photo courtesy of Justin Jones.

beautiful. There were goods baskets, maybe picnic baskets? And there was a patio, where we played, and we drank lemonade all day.

Later on we were afraid to pee, because it burned the cut.

When I walked in, I did see some scissors lying around, there was the smell of the burning needles they use for . . . Probably to disinfect . . . And the remains of what might have been a clitoris, in a basin.

I was too scared, so my sister went first. She's always braver than me. And lucky her, because being the first she couldn't hear the screams of the others.

There were grown-ups also waiting there, but nobody in the room was sad, or happy, it was a normal event for them – well, it wasn't a room, it was a bed attached to the wall.

I had to be dragged in, but my mum gave me some lemon sweets, my favourites. They're still my favourites.

Later . . . we were tied up, so we couldn't move and make the stitches pop out. We were carried to pee, but it hurt badly, so I held it in. My mum said I shouldn't hold it in, that's worse.

My mum never thought she was doing a bad thing. She wanted what all mums want, to promote my . . . marriability, whatever, like any mum in the world. She wanted me to meet a nice man and have a nice family . . . And she had had it done to her, and she was normal, and her mum as well, and so on. It was completely normal to her.

Then we moved to London. One day my period came, and it was very, very painful, we never had paracetamol at home, so I had to put up with the pain. I told my teachers, and they said, 'It's normal to have cramps when you have your period', they'd say, (*in posh accent*) 'You'll be alright'.

My mum said the pain would pass once I had kids. Menstruation's not something you talk about at home.

I was looking after this old lady who had had two kids, and she was still having cramps when her period came – sorry for talking like this, hope this doesn't put you off – so no, it couldn't be just my menstruation. It had to be something else. And besides I couldn't be taking three days off every time I had my . . .

I went to a meeting organised by 'Daughters of Eve', and then I realised what had happened to me. We were all from the same countries, Africa, the Middle East, and we had the same experiences. They recommended that I go to the only clinic that could reverse it in London. So I did, but I didn't tell anyone. I was fully awake during the operation. Well, I was awake the first time too, but in this case they numbed the zone.

I remember going back to Stratford on the train. Now I think, why didn't I get a taxi? So stupid. It's still tricky to go to the loo, it brings back memories.

When you start dating, it's difficult to explain. I mean, I still get pleasure, because not all of my clitoris was removed, but I take more time. I told my current boyfriend after a month and a half, I told him, 'I'm different to the other girls down there', and he was like 'huh', and then he pulls a face like 'ewwww', didn't bother me though, all and all we've been together for six years, but it wasn't easy when we started. Imagine: before this was widely known, some people had been sent to a skin specialist, because doctors didn't know what it was.

I don't mind you telling my story in the play but don't put my name in this, my sister still lives with my parents, and she works in Tesco, so it'd be easy for the people watching the play to recognise her. They might think we're disrespectful, or disloyal. We have some relatives around the house, and she sleeps in the lounge; somebody could break a window with a brick and hurt her. Sometimes that's the kind of abuse we have to face for speaking out.

If this was being done to men, I think it would have been sorted out a long time ago, but since it's done to brown and black girls, we are at the bottom of the list, you know what I mean?

I'm studying to work with children, but I'm scared of the things they do to them . . . I'll wait till I finish my degree and then I'll try for my own babies. I'm about the age, now, what do you think?

I've already chosen the names. I want them to be called Adam and Sarah, because they're intercultural names, Adam is known both in Christianity and Islam, so is Sarah. I also like those names. I think this way they're more likely to be accepted into my family.

They are beautiful names that cross boundaries. Is there anything else you want to know?

Dancing Feet

Bahar Brunton

Characters

Woman 1
Woman 2
Girl
Man

Notes

This play is set in an unspecified location. Female genital mutilation is currently practised in many different countries and the action in this piece could be taking place in any one of them. The set, costumes, accents, etc. should not firmly specify any one country and ideally the cast should be from several different ethnic backgrounds.

A huge celebration is taking place. It surrounds the building and involves the entire community, men as well as women, although the men are unlikely to enter this room.

A large, gaudy sign is hung against the back wall: 'Congratulations'.

Joyous music is heard as two **Women** *appear, singing and dancing. They could be singing along to the Cliff Richard song 'Congratulations' or something more traditional. Not cutters themselves, the women are paid to look after girls who have just been cut.*

Backstage, remove the lid from a bottle of Dettol for the smell.

A young **Girl** *is wheeled in on a makeshift gurney, her eyes closed, legs bound and signs of blood seeping through the sheets.*

Woman 1   First one.

Woman 2   Here she is! I love a party.

Woman 1 (*to* **Girl**)   Are you feeling uncomfortable?

Woman 2   Poor baby.

Woman 1 (*to* **Woman 2**)   Do you have the name?

Woman 2   No.

Woman 1 (*loudly, to* **Girl**)   What is your name, dear? What are you called? Come on. Just first name? (*Shrugs.*) She's not crying. That's something.

Woman 2   No, I don't think she'll cry. Be happy, my lovely. Today has changed your life!

Woman 1   You are a real neat beauty now, eh?

Woman 2   Aw. She's not saying anything. Don't you think you look beautiful? All neat and tidy and feminine. Nice.

Woman 1   Lucky girl. Aren't you? And out of this beauty love will grow. You will have a good husband now and children will flow like water from a tap.

Beat.

But pray for a small baby. (*Laughs.*)

Woman 2   Ah, she's too young to talk about children. Don't trouble her.

Woman 1   She has become a woman.

Woman 2   Yes, technically.

Woman 1   That is what they are now. A lady, ready for your gentleman. Money will shower down on your loved ones, you know. Your loving mother and father. A clean-cut girl is worth more to her husband than a messy minx. Filled with lust from the centre of her brain to the soles of her feet. She will run off with the first man to turn his head in her direction.

Woman 2 (*mocking*) I couldn't help it! It just happened. It was like he could see the real me!

Both laugh.

Woman 2 No, not for you, my love. You will know better than that.

Woman 1 You have been stabilised so that you can be trusted. Full protection. You could even say 'Thank you'.

Woman 2 You will be calm. More appealing, with balanced emotions. And a clean, clean girl.

Woman 1 That is right. It is. Now when you wash you will know that you have removed any trace of mess. Hygiene is absolutely the most important thing. That is something my mother taught me and before that her mother taught her. Remove the grit so that your body can flower. Even my daughter, already, she is dirt-free.

Woman 2 Soap and water are not always enough.

*The **Girl**'s legs begin to shake.*

Woman 2 Oh, oh. She's wetting the bed. Oh dear. (*To* **Girl**.) Not your fault.

Woman 1 You'll have to get used to that.

Woman 2 No, no. Possibly not. Not everyone. Or not every night. And how is your little girl? All fine now?

Woman 1 (*briskly*) Yes, yes. Completely recovered. That's it.

Woman 2 I really am pleased.

Beat.

Sure?

Silence.

(*Looking at* **Girl**.) She's really going to need new clothes. Is there anything for her to wear?

Woman 1 I don't know. We keep a few things.

Woman 2 (*to* **Girl**) Well, then, would you like to choose, my baby?

Woman 1 (*tutting*) She is not a baby!

Woman 2 (*smiling*) (*to* **Girl**) If you show me your teeth then the world will be happy. Maybe we should leave her for a moment?

Woman 1 (*gritting her teeth*) My dear, no. We are not paid to leave her. You stay here.

Woman 2 Have we been paid yet?

Woman 1 We will be. It's good business.

Beat.

So come on. You? Is there any joy for you?

Woman 2 (*gestures towards her stomach*)   Er, no. Not yet.

Woman 1   It will be soon. I am sure of that. (*To* **Girl**.) Your family will want to hear words from you, remember. I was chatty as the birds. So many questions.

Woman 2   So much to look forward to. I have heard that it increases good health by up to one hundred per cent!

Woman 1   Yes, that may be true. It's almost certainly a fact. (*To* **Girl**.) Now come now. That is enough. Do you really want your mummy to see you like this? We need smiling! In three weeks, four weeks, you can jump up and sing!

Woman 2   Don't try and jump. No jumping at first. And no running.

Woman 1   Yes, OK. That's right. See you can walk properly first. Then all of this will be over, and you will feel so happy. (*Looks towards the door.*) All of your friends will be happy too.

Woman 2   Then you, your mummy, your daddy and everyone can travel all the way back home again. You can go back to your parks and your cafés, and be a good girl from now on.

Woman 1   You are being a good girl right now.

Woman 2   Brave.

Woman 1   Obedient. Like she should be. Although she refuses to speak.

Woman 2   Poor thing.

Woman 1   Make her!

Woman 2   All your friends at school will be so jealous of your holiday when they hear about it . . .

Woman 1 *shakes her head.*

Woman 1 (*to* **Woman 2**)   This is not spoken about. Ever.

Woman 2   No? . . . Sorry, sorry.

Woman 1 (*to* **Girl**)   You know, maybe don't tell if someone asks you about anything.

Woman 2   People you don't know – outside the family . . .

Woman 1   They won't understand.

Woman 2 (*to* **Woman 1**)   Do you think she's listening?

Woman 1   She must listen. She has to learn!

Woman 2 (*to* **Girl**)   Come on, now. Can you hear me? Look up . . .

Pause. As they stand quietly distant sounds of the party can be heard.

Listen!

3 From left: Shuna Snow (Woman 1) and Stephanie Yamson (Woman 2) in *Dancing Feet*. Theatre503, London, 21 August 2014. Photo courtesy of John Wilson.

The **Women** *resume their singing and dancing, at first directing their actions towards the* **Girl***, trying to cheer her up and provoke a response. Then, caught up in the moment, the two* **Women** *dance together.*

From the side of the stage a **Man** *dances his way towards them, singing along. He is caught up in the moment and doesn't realise that he has wandered into* this *part of the building. He comes quite far into the room but when he sees the* **Girl** *he stops, turns around and leaves, unwilling to deal with the reality of it. As he walks off, he starts singing along with and dancing towards somebody offstage.*

Woman 1 *looks away as soon as he leaves.* **Woman 2***'s gaze lingers on the* **Man** *for a few moments longer before she turns back to the* **Girl***.*

Woman 2   No wonder he doesn't look – this part is always unpleasant.

Woman 1   So what? What else can be done? We cut them, they will cut the next ones.

Woman 2   Of course – I'm not saying there's any other way.

Woman 1   This is done as it has always been done, and it must carry on. Otherwise who are we?

Woman 2   Don't know.

Beat.

Woman 1   Let's hope they hurry up out there and get through them nice and quick today.

Woman 2   Really? (*To* **Girl***, reassuring her.*) I don't mind being here.

Woman 1   I have guests coming to dinner. Very important people.

Woman 2   Your in-laws?

Woman 1   Yes.

Woman 2   Still. We mustn't rush them. Let them do it properly, with a steady hand.

Beat.

I know what this girl needs. She wants her presents! Don't worry, we haven't forgotten them.

Woman 1   I'm sure your parents will come in with an armful of things for you.

Woman 2 (*to* **Girl**)   Ooh. What do you think you're going to get? What could it be?

Woman 1   What about a teddy bear? A nice little teddy just for you?

Woman 2   Oh, don't be silly. Look at her! She's too old for bears.

Woman 1 (*firmly*)   Well, I had a teddy and I loved it.

Woman 2   I don't think girls these days still play with toys at her age.

Woman 1   And how would you know?

Woman 2 (*softly*)   I wouldn't know. (*To* **Girl**.) I'm sure you can have a toy if you still want one.

Woman 1   She might.

Woman 2   I've got it. What you want, darling, is a nice pair of shoes. Something really pretty and sweet. Maybe a small heel?

Woman 1 (*rolling her eyes*)   Really!

Woman 2   Hang on. Wait now, I think . . . Is she asleep?

Woman 1   Is she? Oh yes. I think so.

Woman 2   I'm sure her mother will be here soon.

Woman 1 (*shrugs*)   This is no place for a mother. What parent wants to see their child like this?

Beat.

Trust me. When she has snapped out of it, they will come.

Woman 2   She doesn't look all that good.

Woman 1   They never do. Why would they? All that she's been through today. I have seen plenty that look worse than this.

Woman 2   I don't know . . .

Woman 1   I've seen ones with their vomit all over them. In their hair, in their clothes. On my clothes. They have thrown up from the pain. We have nothing to stop it hurting.

Woman 2   Why nothing?

Woman 1 (*shrugs*)   There is nothing.

Woman 2   Nothing at all. (*Sighs, frustrated.*) God. (*She leans towards the* **Girl***.*) Well done for not throwing up, little girl. You're real grown-up. You can handle anything now. Well done. Well done. (*To* **Woman 1***.*) How many girls do you think you have seen here?

Woman 1 (*shrugs*)   How many? I don't count. A large number, I suppose.

Woman 2   You have done this for many years?

Woman 1   As will you.

Woman 2   I'm wondering how many I must have seen already.

Beat.

Woman 1   Why are you asking this? Just care for them and then they leave. Another one takes their place. Another handful of coins for looking after them.

Pause.

Woman 2   Tell me – do you remember it, when it happened to you?

Woman 1   I don't know.

Woman 2   Yes you do, surely?

Woman 1   No. We don't talk about this in front of her.

Woman 2   She is asleep. How old were you?

Woman 1 (*sighs*)   Why? Oh my! All these questions. I was six and a half.

Woman 2   So you think of it?

Woman 1 *nods.*

Woman 2   I can't remember. I must have been a very young baby. Still in my mother's arms, I'm assuming. My family is silent. They don't tell me anything at all.

Woman 1   You must have been very young, yes. Otherwise you would not forget it. There's no need to think.

Woman 2   I imagine that I cried. Still a baby, very little. But a woman like my mama. And I can't have a baby.

Woman 1   No.

Woman 2   Something happened, I suppose. During. Or after.

Beat.

And long before I could speak.

Beat.

There's no changing it now. I am sure you had already realised that. Did you?

Woman 1   Sssshhhhhhhhhhh!

Woman 2   Yes.

Beat.

Woman 2 (*louder*)   Does it feel like there's a fire when you urinate?

Woman 1   I'm not going to . . . I don't want to talk about this!

Woman 2   Nobody does. I might be the only one.

Woman 1 (*quietly*)   Don't be a fool. You know that you're not.

Pause.

Woman 2 (*to* **Girl**)   It can be hard being a woman. A real woman. It can be a nasty business.

Woman 1   Just briefly. You move on.

Woman 2   But at least you can't shame your husband. The cut has protected him and he will love you for it.

Woman 1   You are such a lucky girl. Now you can go home and concentrate on your studies. Not all parents do this for their daughters, you know.

Woman 2   Or maybe your grandparents? Grandmother?

Woman 1   It could be.

Woman 2   Somebody loves you.

Beat.

Woman 1   You have done the right thing. Had the right thing done. Sometimes a girl will be left whole, left to look like a baby. And to act like one too. Selfish. Always thinking about themselves and what they want to have next. Who will want to talk to them? While everyone else is learning, you want to be the one to remain dumb? You will look at these girls and you will want to laugh because they are so different.

Woman 2   I'm sure that you will have a happier life. The best life possible.

The **Girl** *starts to shiver.*

Woman 2   Shouldn't we get something more to cover her with?

Woman 1   It is much too hot in here for her to be cold. (*Loudly to* **Girl**.) It is very hot!

Woman 2   Even her hands are warm.

Woman 1   There. You see? (*To* **Girl**.) You don't have to worry any more. It's done. This happens once and only once. Soon you will have been a woman for a whole day. Then two days a woman, three days. And before you have noticed the time pass you will be old like me. But still a woman.

The **Girl** *continues to tremble.*

Woman 2   She's been quiet for too long. This is not right. She's too hot! Too hot!

Woman 1   If she is on fire it is because she is meant to burn. These things . . . sometimes . . . happen.

After a while the shaking stops.

Woman 2   Oh! Please no!

Beat.

Woman 1   Ugh. First thing in the morning.

They cover the **Girl***'s face with a sheet.*

Woman 2   Oh!

Woman 1   Go on. Get her out of here. There's another one coming. Another new lady. Right, right.

Woman 2 *wipes her eyes.*

The **Girl** *is wheeled out of the room as the* **Women** *turn to the entrance. They begin to sing and dance once again in anticipation of the next arrival.*

Lights go down.

Mutant

Karis E. Halsall

Characters

Safa
Dr Chaudhry
Mother

Notes

Any text in brackets is unspoken and included only to clarify the meaning of the rest of the line
– An unfinished thought
/ An interruption
(beat) indicates a beat or small pause

Stage left, **Safa**, *fourteen, stands, in her school uniform.*

Upstage, and slightly to the left, **Dr Chaudhry** *looms.*

Safa   On the last day of term,
No one's really listening, are they?
Everyone's daydreaming.
And I'm no exception.
Dreaming about staying out in the park till late and it
Still not being dark
And the smell of rain on hot pavements
And new-cut grass.
And
I'm thinking about the twinkle of
Ice-cream vans,
And getting my bike out of the shed
and water fights with Danny
and getting to see Danny every day.
And just Danny
in general,
really.

Dr Chaudhry   My father always tells the story of how he arrived in London.
Nineteen, and with nothing but the equivalent of five pounds in his pocket
And a note from his previous employer
saying he was a 'good boy'.
Back in those days, everyone would say,
head to Brick Lane –
But my father would reply
'I've just left home, I'm not looking to go back there anytime soon'
My father worked hard, he built his business from scratch and made England
his home.
So because of him, I've always felt British.
And if anyone ever tried to tell me otherwise, Dad would say –
'This is Britain.
And Britain is a nation built on multiculturalism.'

Safa   And I think he likes me too,
Cause –
Sometimes when I make him laugh.
He smiles at me like, like this smile I've never seen him give
Anyone else.

Dr Chaudhry   As far back as we have written history, we have invasions,
Diasporas
Wars.
New cultures
descending on this small isle
And trying to

thrash out cultural identities,
With new and exotic hybrids emerging.

Safa's **Mother** *emerges, and stands, slightly removed from the action.*

Safa   But Dad would never go for it.
Cause Danny's not,
You know.
(*beat*)
Like us.

Dr Chaudhry   In Britain we're tolerant.
I mean,
We don't just tolerate, do we?
We embrace!
We embrace multiculturalism –

Safa   Miss Baker catches me daydreaming.
She says 'Safa's away with the fairies again'
And then asks me to tell the class
What an oxymoron is.
And I think about last week.
The fight with Mum.
When.
Out of nowhere she said:

Mother   It's your only choice

Safa   'Only choice'
What an oxymoron.

Dr Chaudhry   Multiculturalism
In itself – can only successfully occur
when we tackle ignorance.
And move towards a
true understanding of our
opposing cultural constructs.
(*beat*)
Not surrendering to the hegemony
On either side –

Safa   I use it as an example.
Miss Baker seems pleased.
She says I'm 'insightful'.
And when the bell goes for the last time that year
I sprint home,
Undoing my tie as I go,
Ready to
Throw my bag
on the sofa

And not look at it again till
At least a week before term starts.

Dr Chaudhry   I'm not trying to defend myself but –
Within any ethnic diaspora
Existing within a nation of mixed creed and race,
There are likely to be traditions,
Practices
Which perhaps don't fit within our cultural understanding.

Safa   As I round the corner onto my road,
I slow my sprint down
Cause Mum's always saying:

Mother   Safa! Stop rushing around.

Safa   She worries.
Thinks one day I'm gonna trip and fall
And end up getting hurt.

Dr Chaudhry   And there has to be some level of sensitivity towards that –

Safa   At first I don't really notice
There's three cars
In the drive.

4 From left: Shuna Snow (Mother), Shalini Peiris (Safa) and Chin Nyenwe (Dr Chaudhry) in *Mutant*. Theatre503, London, 21 August 2014. Photo courtesy of John Wilson.

Dad's home from work early –
And Auntie Rumi is here?
Three cars in the drive
(*beat*)
One
I don't recognise.
As I reach my gate
The feeling in my gut gets worse,
I get this sense that [something's not right]
(*beat*)
Like the beginning of something.
And the end too.
(*beat*)
But I go in.
Like my feet make the decision for me.

Dr Chaudhry   What one has to understand is that
The indoctrination runs very deeply.

Safa   I enter the house as gently as possible.
Instinctually, I want to call out
'Mum'.
But my body knows better than that
The word stays stuck in my throat.
Which catches the smell of cigarette smoke.
The smell of my dad.
Overpowering.
He's in the kitchen,
Door shut.
Silent.
I gently open the door
to the front room.
And I realise –
She doesn't look like how I'd imagined her.
She looks all soft.
Not like the monster I had pictured
in my head.

Dr Chaudhry   I fear that with all the recent media attention,
The sensationalism
The vilification of it /

Safa   I look to my family,
In the hope that I'm wrong.

Dr Chaudhry   Perhaps without open discussion
All we're really doing is
Driving the practice further underground –

Safa   But Mum's face
(*beat*)
Blank.

Dr Chaudhry   And when we have women who attend Harley Street
And actively pay for type II,

Safa   Auntie's face
(*beat*)
Blank.

Dr Chaudhry   I mean who are we really to –

Safa   The smell of smoke.

Dr Chaudhry   Isn't it kind of arrogant of us?
Isn't it?

Safa   A family gathering.
They want it to feel like a rite of passage.
(*beat*)
It feels like a funeral –
The wedding with no pictures.

Dr Chaudhry   I was making my pre-natal preparations.

Safa   I catch her making her preparations
So I close my eyes,

Dr Chaudhry   My first thought on seeing her was –

Safa   But in my fright,
My senses come alive
And
I can smell hot metal now,

Dr Chaudhry   'What kind of animal could have done this to her?'

Safa   It smells like fear.

Dr Chaudhry   I thought she'd been mauled.

Safa   Suddenly I'm five again
And Mum's piercing my ears
And I tell myself,
It's no different
It's no different
But it is
Different.

Dr Chaudhry   Of course I was aware of the practice but –
I've never actually undertaken any training on it.

Safa   Stale smoke and hot metal.

Dr Chaudhry   I've been with the private sector for six years now.
And in all my time I'd never seen –
Anything.
Anything
[Like it.]

Safa   And in the midst of the panic and the fear
I hear Mum say:

Mother   Be brave, Safa,

Safa   'Be brave'.
Those words,
Try and drive them out,
shake them off,
But they repeat endlessly.

Mother   You must be brave.

Dr Chaudhry   The size of the [hole] that was left –
I mean there was no way [she could have given birth] –

Safa   I want to scream,

Dr Chaudhry   An incision had to be made then,
Obviously
To open her up.

Safa   'Teach me how to be brave, Mum.
Stand up for me.'

Dr Chaudhry   She was only twenty-one.
A wisp of a thing.
Her husband.
Much older.
And from the few, quiet words she spoke
I could tell she was English.
He made it very clear to me,
that if I didn't make the post-natal adjustments he was expecting.
Then.
I mean.
You must understand –
These people –

Safa   Mum's face,
(*beat*)
turned away
Auntie's face,
(*beat*)
approaching
The smell of smoke.

I am held down,
My aunt's knees in my chest.
Keeping me still.

Dr Chaudhry   They're inexperienced
Using unsterilised apparatus not fit for surgical use /

Safa   As that woman
Slices right into my

Dr Chaudhry   Often they don't manage to perform the procedure in one go /

Safa   She slices right into my

Dr Chaudhry   It's all very poorly done /

Safa   Right into my

Pause.

Soul.

The sound I make
Could curdle blood.

Long pause.

It takes me two weeks before I can go to the toilet again,
Without it feeling like acid [on the wound].
Mum carries me back and forth from my bed,
Whenever I need to go.
I can't stand or stretch my legs out.
A horrible sting.
Hard not to cry every time.
She bathes me in warm salt water
So I don't get infected.
She sings to me,
Brushes my hair behind my ear
I always feel so small.
I want to hide away,
My body was confusing enough before.

I wonder if she ever suffered like me.
I wonder when she hears my howls in the night
If she ever thinks twice –

When I finally get the courage to look at myself.
I see carnage.
I see myself ravaged.
I feel like a mutant.
Everything down there is unrecognizable.

Doesn't even feel like my skin.
Mangled. Sore.
The only thing that's left of me.
Is my birthmark, that's shaped like a flower.
I want to scratch and scratch until I tear it off.
I used to think it was beautiful.
Now it's the ugliest thing I've ever seen.

I can never grow back from this.
I know that.
I wonder what kind of man might find this attractive.

Dr Chaudhry   I assessed the risk to my patient.
And I deemed it to be a sizeable risk.
If I hadn't done it,
then he'd have employed someone less qualified than me to do it.

Safa   I think about Danny.
I haven't spoken to him since. I don't think I ever will.
I see him look at me sadly from his bedroom window sometimes
But I know if he knew
He could never love [a mutant].

Dr Chaudhry   I took decisive action.
I stitched her back up, yes
As I would with any other patient with tearing.
(*beat*)
I decided to put in a suture to stop the bleeding.
(*beat*)
It was only a slight [adjustment] –

Pause.

This? This is a quibble about a couple of stitches.
After a series of systematic failures that left me in the firing line.
And it's a . . .
A distraction.

Safa   Now I'm ready for marriage.
They say.
Like anyone's ever really ready for anything.
I wanted to go to university.
I wanted –
I wanted to be 'insightful'.
I wanted a life for myself.
I suppose it was never about what I wanted. Sometimes I wonder though.
If this is my life.
Then,
Surely.

Surely there must be another choice?

Silence.

Dr Chaudhry   The thing that will never leave me.
The thing that's embedded in my memory
Sitting there, as if just sort of placed on her right thigh
Was a birthmark shaped just like a daisy.
So perfect, and so delicate. Something about it.
She flinched. Almost ashamed that I'd seen it.
That's stuck with me.
Of all the things she could have been ashamed that I'd seen.

Silence.

We can't –

We can't just pretend this isn't happening.

Interview with Melissa Dean and Alex Crampton, producer and director of *Little Stitches*

Daniela Cavallaro and Claire Kennedy

How did the show originate?

Alex   The idea for the show came from Melissa; she felt strongly that FGM was something that needed to be talked about more, and she set the project in motion.

Melissa   At the time, I was primarily an actress wanting to stage work I cared about so that I could tell important stories and act too. So, in 2013 I started BAREtruth Theatre Company. Through writers' groups on Facebook I put out a call for submission of plays about human rights issues, and hundreds of people sent me emails with plays attached. Raúl [Raúl Quirós Molina], who came to run the company with me, looked through these plays alongside me, but nothing seemed quite right for us.

At the time I had joined a scheme called The Prince's Trust, a charity that helps people under the age of thirty develop the necessary skills to start their own businesses. I was assigned a business adviser, Richard Harding, and I explained to him what I wanted to do with my theatre company. Richard had been working with me for a couple of months when one day he asked if I had seen an article in the *Guardian* about FGM, suggesting that it might be an issue I could do something with. I read the article and was extremely moved by it. I started to investigate the issue more deeply and then, in consultation with Raúl, decided that FGM would be a perfect fit for our first project.

I didn't end up acting in *Little Stitches* as there was so much work involved for me as producer. Our funding bid was unsuccessful which meant I wasn't able to pay someone to split the work with me. So I had to take it on full time, over a period of six months. I wasn't doing any other work at the time, which was extremely helpful, and I was living with my parents – I couldn't have done it without their support.

What made you decide to put four short plays together, instead of creating just one longer one?

Melissa   We chose to have four plays because of the headline I read in that first article in the *Guardian*: 'In the UK, an estimated 137,000 women are living with the consequences of female genital mutilation.' There were so many stories to tell, how could we tell just one? We thought it would be more interesting for audiences to hear four different points of view. The four plays told very different stories.

Through our research, we learned that FGM has been carried out in the UK for a long time and campaigners had been trying to raise the issue with successive governments and the press for twenty-five years without much success. However, the article in the *Guardian* gained a lot of attention and then other media outlets started reporting on it. This is an extract from our press release about the show:

> Today the BAREtruth Theatre Company announces the world première of *Little Stitches*, an evening of four plays each tackling the subject of female genital mutilation. More than 140 million women and girls worldwide have suffered

FGM, and, although the huge majority of victims live in Africa and certain Middle Eastern and Asian countries, the number of cases in the UK is on the rise. An estimated 137,000 women in Britain are living with the consequences of FGM, and more than 20,000 girls under the age of fifteen are thought to be at risk each year. However, despite FGM having been criminalized in the UK nearly thirty years ago, there has only been a single prosecution.

How did you choose the writers?

Melissa   I contacted Karis Halsall, a writer I had worked with previously. She had been one of the playwrights involved in my showcase at the Oxford School of Drama during my final year of studying there. I loved her work. I have always thought she is an exceptional writer. So it was a no-brainer to ask her! I already knew Raúl as we were running BAREtruth together. When starting up the company, I had put out a call on various arts websites to find someone to run it with me. I had interviewed about ten people, but Raúl had stood out as someone who genuinely cared about what I wanted to do. He also had a real passion for theatre and writing and I thought we would make a good team, which we did. Bahar Brunton was recommended by Raúl; he knew her and her work well. Isley Lynn was one of the writers who had replied to my call for playscripts. I went to see her play *Skin a Cat* at a venue in London, and met her afterwards for a good chat. I just loved her work, I thought she was a very strong writer with a bold, unique voice.

Each of the four plays focuses on a different aspect of FGM/C. How did you arrive at the selection of themes and characters?

Melissa   I explained to the writers that we wanted to create four short pieces about FGM that focused on different aspects of the issue. I found out about various FGM events going on in London for us to attend, such as an Amnesty International event featuring an excellent line-up of speakers and poets. I also did a great deal of reading of newspaper articles and other material, and put all the documents into a shared online folder as a resource for the writers to draw on. Using that material, as well as their own research, which included attending events, the writers then came up with their ideas and proposed them to both Raúl and me.

It happened quite naturally that they each chose a different approach to the issue. We never had the problem of saying 'These two plays are similar; can you change that?' Each writer had their own style and specific aspects that they wanted to work on.

Raúl was the only writer who wanted to create a verbatim theatre piece. He and I went to meet a famous writer/actor called Robin Soans, who had written some verbatim theatre and kindly gave us some tips.

What sort of research did you do when developing the play? What kinds of people did you speak to?

Melissa   In the 2014 production, we partnered with Manor Gardens Welfare Trust, who run a campaign to end FGM. I wanted the entire team – writers, actors, the director and myself – to receive some advice on how to talk about FGM, and how to deal with such a sensitive subject which affects so many women's lives. One of the nurses from Manor Gardens gave a presentation for us and answered our many questions.

I also contacted every single FGM organization there is, and told them what we were hoping to do, asking if they would put us in touch with any communities where we might be able to interview women who had been victims of FGM. Most didn't reply, which is understandable given it is such a delicate, and personal, subject. But some did, and they put us in touch with community centres and charities in various areas of London, who in turn helped us make contact with women who were willing to talk to us. Eventually we interviewed seven women, and Raúl used a lot of what they said in his verbatim piece.

In the East London borough of Newham, we attended an awareness event about child marriage and FGM and learned a great deal about the facts and figures of abuse against women, child marriage and honour killings in the borough of Newham alone. The statistics were awful and shocking. It was unbelievable to learn about these things happening, today, in the city where I live, and that little or nothing was being done to prevent them.

I also set up a collective interview at a primary school, with a group of Muslim women who were mothers of children there and friends. None of them wanted to speak, initially, and neither Raúl nor I knew how to start talking about such a subject. And that became the title of Raúl's play: 'Where Do I Start?' You can't begin with, 'So have you all been cut?' In the same way, if you were talking to a rape survivor, you wouldn't open with, 'So tell us about the rape.' But this being new to us, it was tricky. So I'm pretty sure we just began with, 'Where are you from, each of you?'

It was easier conducting individual interviews. One was with a twenty-two-year-old woman from Somalia. Initially she was very nervous, but once she got talking about her childhood she seemed to relax. She spoke about the civil war in Somalia, and seeing the dead lying in the streets. She talked very easily about FGM – we didn't have to ask her much – and how she went with a group of other girls to have this 'ceremony' done to her. FGM is often referred to as a celebration – the day you become a woman, a ceremony. She became one of the main characters in Raúl's play.

Alex A lot of research had been done, by the writers and Melissa, before I joined the process. And they had already carried out quite a few revisions of the scripts. I did some last-minute dramaturgy work, together with the writers, asking questions and tidying things up a bit. But by and large, the content was already fixed.

While we were rehearsing, Melissa organized for Leyla Hussein and Dexter Dias QC to come and talk with us. Leyla has been through FGM herself, and she does a lot of FGM-awareness-raising activities in her community. She made a documentary for Channel 4 here in the UK called *The Cruel Cut*. I think you can watch it online.[1] Dexter is a human rights lawyer who has been fighting FGM for a very long time. We all had a lot of questions, and Leyla talked to us about her experience as an FGM survivor and the more physical, biological aspects of what is involved. We all watched *The Cruel Cut* and read several case studies. I think first of all it was about getting up to speed on

---

1 The documentary was released in 2013. A preview can be viewed at https://www.youtube.com/watch?v=rBV1zKft3oY.

what the different types of procedure are, and where they are practised. Dexter and Leyla were particularly helpful in demystifying a few aspects – clearing up some muddy perceptions of the practice as being related to ethnicity or religion or culture, and myths you hear such as, 'It's Islamic.' And Dexter had interesting things to say about the practice being a response to parental insecurity, and how that might stem from escaping a war zone, for example.

That kind of discussion was also important in preparing us to talk to audiences. And we were planning to hold free outreach performances in libraries and community centres, to be followed by question-and-answer sessions. We felt it was important for us all to be well briefed on the broad cultural issues, on what's true and what's not true, and on misconceptions around the whole practice.

With respect to the direction and staging, there were some specific topics we needed to learn about and think about for each play.

For Isley Lynn's play, *Sleight of Hand*, the preparation for staging had to do with the world building: developing the world of the characters, mapping out how they intersected with each other, and getting an idea of the kind of community they were involved in. And, for example, we had to find out about the rituals, and the reasons behind the cutting 'season' – because the schoolgirl character in that play would be flying to her home country at a certain time of year. We needed to learn that girls would be sent home at that time, and what that entailed for diaspora communities. We read quite a few papers published online by organizations that were campaigning for an end to FGM and child marriage – papers that gave information on the pressures that cultures face, that communities face, in sending their kids back home.

For Raúl Quirós Molina's piece, *Where Do I Start?*, in particular, we learned about the medical side of FGM. We were looking into the physiological aspect of type III and type I practices and their differences. Leyla gave us a lot of information, including on how they affect urination and periods. That gave us a bit more of a grasp of the physical reality of FGM.

The work that stands out, in terms of our need for preparation, is Bahar Brunton's *Dancing Feet*. It is almost dreamlike, and we decided to go for something of a supernatural, otherworldly setting. There was a journey we wanted to capture in the progression of the plays, and with this one, the third in the sequence, we were going deeper into the heart of the issue and things got more subjective and expressive. It felt a little bit more . . . I'm going to say 'dangerous', because we were actually representing on stage a girl who has been cut and the women who look after the girls after the procedure. We – the whole team – were wary of making any sweeping cultural assumptions, of generalizing inappropriately, in our representation of those women characters. We wanted to capture the specificity of FGM, to acknowledge how its practice is affected by religion, race, culture and ethnicity.

So, we defined the first minder specifically as an older Egyptian woman, and did a lot of research on accent, for example. I found a documentary that focused on some Egyptian women who cut – we were watching every documentary we could – and we drew on that for models of mannerisms and physicality for the actor, Shuna Snow. We placed the other woman, if I remember correctly, as coming from somewhere in the Horn of Africa, another area where type III was the prevailing form of FGM. This was also about identifying the girl in the scene, who dies. If you're going to die from the procedure then it's going to be the most extreme version, so we needed to consider where that is practised. So we wanted to capture the kind of pandemic nature of FGM, by trying to be specific in setting and characterization, but also capture a universal nightmarish quality of it.

That play is also quite risky, I guess, in the way that it uses humour. So it was the staging of that one that made me most nervous. But, weirdly, I think it really does something quite different from the others. I think it is the dark edge to this particular text that makes it so special. It really goes to the space where this act takes place, and not in just a physical sense but in an almost metaphysical sense. In its surreal and symbolic nature, it captures something of the collective pain of this practice, but without blaming anybody. It seeks to understand the conversations, the motivations and the self-repression that cause these women to do this to each other. It's humane in its understanding, or in its seeking to understand. There's a lot of attention to blame in public discourse around the issue of FGM, and that won't heal anything. So the daring of Bahar's piece – to go to that dark place, without judgement – has a healing quality to it.

You mentioned a progression: is the sequence of the four plays in the performance important?

Alex   Yes, the order of the four plays is very important. We decided to create a journey, starting from the outskirts of the issue: all these people, all these members of the community who have a hunch that something's going on but they're not sure. So, starting from the fringes – with respect to the girls who are at the heart of it – and then coming a bit closer, to the medical professionals who are let in a bit on what is happening. Then to the minders who work with the cutters. Finishing up with the primary voice, the protagonist's voice, the girl herself: we are in the moment of her coming home from school and knowing this thing is going to happen. So we wanted to take the audience on a journey in time and perspective, from the periphery, to something that *might* be happening, to *that* person in *that* moment.

Melissa   The order of the plays was a directorial choice. The show ends with Karis Halsall's *Mutant*, which is a series of alternating monologues by a doctor and a young girl. The writing makes you reflect, because the doctor pleads with the listener to hear his point of view: that he felt he was cornered, with no other choice. He has to fight his case, so we hear, and possibly empathize with, a viewpoint we may not have been expecting to connect with. That is what good storytelling is about – challenging us to hear all sides. It's a thought-provoking end to the show.

In the performance, did the same actors play several roles over the four plays?

Alex   Yes, and it was partly a budgetary matter: why employ a cast of twenty, when we could just use the same actors in multiple roles? But it also meant we could concentrate all the familiarity with the material and the research that we'd done. And, from a theatrical point of view, we could showcase the virtuosity and flexibility of a great cast, who could chop and change between different roles and different nationalities. It demanded a lot of accent work because, again, we didn't want to generalize, or merely approximate the accents; they all needed to be recognizable and specific.

Getting ready for the casting was quite a bit of work: figuring out how we could piece it all together and what the casting call was – what minimum number of actors we could get away with, and what the combinations of roles would be.

Melissa   On the casting team, in addition to Alex, Raúl and me, there was Emma Deegan, the assistant director. We had considerable debate over the casting. For example, we auditioned a very young actress who hadn't had much, if any, acting experience. She was a survivor of FGM and auditioned brilliantly, with clear emotional connection to one of the pieces. But when you're choosing an actor to play multiple roles, they have to be rounded, capable of diving into the language, the energy, the heartbeat of each of the roles. I felt that this actor's lack of experience and lack of training meant she was not quite in a position to do that. She would certainly have been capable of playing the character Felicity in Raúl's piece, *Where Do I Start?*, but I didn't think she could sit comfortably in the other roles.

A separate debate came up over race following the auditions. We wanted our cast to be a mirror of the multitude of races involved in the world of FGM: Asian, white, black, mixed race. I remember an excellent white British actress who was in her mid-twenties. She auditioned wearing a scarf around her head and speaking with a Turkish accent. She wanted us to forget that she had blonde hair and an English accent, and to see her Middle Eastern heritage. But we couldn't justify having a young white English actress in the show. Again, it wouldn't work for the multiple roles.

We needed to cast only five actors and had to be thorough and rigid in that process. It was essential for us to be confident that each actor cast could play a variety of roles and be right for the parts. In the end, the only white British actor we cast was Shuna Snow, who was older than the rest of the cast and had a lot of experience. Shuna can really connect with language and tell a story. She was captivating to watch and, when she played one of the African minders of girls who have been cut, she was so good you forgot about the colour of her skin and really engaged with her acting.

Once rehearsals began, we became a close team, and everyone bonded well. The same happened the following year, when we staged a second production, with a slightly different cast. I'm extremely grateful to all the actors for the love, effort and talent they put into *Little Stitches*.

Can you tell us about the costumes, set, lighting and sound design?

Alex   In the creative team we had: Anna Sbokou, who I've worked with a lot, as lighting designer; Anna Privitera creating the set; Erik Medeiros, another person I've worked with a lot, on sound design; and Fiona Lockton on costume design. For the set, Anna Privitera came up with a half-exposed steel-frame construction, like a cage structure. There wasn't a lot of action in the show, everything was a bit still, with talking heads, except in Bahar's piece. But we didn't want just the characters sitting on stools and talking, we wanted to give a changing, evolving sense of space. So Anna devised this steel construction, to create a sense of three different rooms, to compartmentalize the stage.

The two Annas worked closely together and one of the initial images they came up with was of vertical, suspended neon strips; they were inspired by the strip lighting in the aisle of a plane. And the cage, which also represented the restrictions on the girls, could mask the strip lighting and give us various different effects and glows as we moved through the play. Again, there was a progression: alongside the journey in the plays there was a journey in the lighting. It was most expansive in the opening piece *Sleight of Hand*, with general cover and five spots on the five characters, and then restricted down as we moved through the sequence. In *Dancing Feet* things got gloomier; we pulled the action out of the cage, moving it downstage to where a girl lay wrapped in a blanket on a dirty mattress. In the final piece, *Mutant*, we had three compartments for the three characters, but with Safa able to move further downstage. So, yes, we wanted variation in look and feel, we didn't want it to be too static and talky. Given the very simple but suggestive design, we needed to work a little bit harder in order to obtain such variation.

For the costumes we created mood boards, picture boards, for all the pieces, to get a different feel for each. Again, *Dancing Feet* was hard because we were trying to pull some motifs or references from the Horn of Africa and Egypt but the play wasn't exactly set in one particular space. It was a lot easier to design the outfits for *Sleight of Hand*.

Given that everyone was role swapping, the costumes had to be easily put on and taken off. Actually, during the first performance, at Theatre503, the transitions between the four plays took ages, and there was feedback: 'Guys you've gotta speed this up!' So after that we were drilling! I think the first transition was the busiest, and everyone had to know exactly what they were doing.

We had carpet panels on the set for the first play, *Sleight of Hand*, to create a classroom area for the teacher's voice. There were some movable parts to the set, to give some variation in texture and feel. It was as if the stage was deconstructing as we were moving towards the end, where we wanted things to be a bit stripped down and suggestive.

A major aspect of Erik's work was creating the sound in between the pieces, and that was meant to accentuate this sort of distorted journey, going deeper into the dark heart of the issue that we were talking about. His soundscape related to the girl in the last piece, *Mutant*, the character Safa. It was made up of sounds she could have been hearing outside the classroom at the start of that piece, like planes taking off, and feet running around outside. The soundscape began in the first transition but would get a bit more distorted at each of the later transitions. Between *Dancing Feet* and *Mutant*, a weird kind of merry-go-round thread would creep into it, and there was a bit more distortion and then suddenly, snap, we were in a much more realistic space. We were in the classroom, and we could hear those things going on outside, and then the bell rang and that landed us in the room.

So, overall, there was a long, slow, reverse collapse into that last piece, and we were aiming to frame that with all those production elements, those design elements.

What forms of publicity did you use?

Melissa   The three theatres that we worked in with the first production were Theatre503, the Gate Theatre and the Arcola Theatre Tent. When I met with the artistic director of the Gate Theatre, he said he wouldn't be willing to bring *Little Stitches* in unless we had an excellent public relations team on board. He recommended Kate Morley, who does public relations for many West End shows. So I contacted her and told her: 'I don't have any funding, I'm paying for this myself, what will your fee be?' She came on board right away. 'Melissa,' she said, 'I think this is going to do amazingly well in the press because it's such a big topic right now and no one else has talked about it.' We were the first theatre company to stage a play about FGM in London, or in England, as far as I know. Kate obtained amazing publicity. The *Guardian*, whose article had provided the original stimulus for the plays, did a double-page spread on us, and local newspapers interviewed the writers and director. We also received really good reviews once we opened, including in *The Times* and the *Evening Standard* – lots of four-star reviews.

We put together a fundraising campaign to raise £12,000 to pay our team, at minimum union rates, and gain traction for the show. We made a video featuring various people reading lines from Raúl's play, as well as the voice of a young girl from one of our interviews. We pushed it on social media platforms, asking friends and family to share it and to donate. This turned out to be an effective way of publicizing the play, as there were many shares and retweets.

We also printed flyers and posters and decorated half of London with them. We distributed them to various venues, cafés and theatres in the city. The three theatres also did their own advertising through mailing lists and their websites.

How was the staging of Little Stitches *different in the libraries, compared with the theatres?*

Alex   In the libraries there was no staging; it was very much a pared-down rehearsed reading. We didn't have those technical framings – the lights and sound. Given that the libraries and community spaces were often very small, and we'd set up five chairs and have all the actors sitting there, it was really a case of talking heads. But this meant that all the attention could be concentrated on the material; it was good to have a version of the performance that was distilled and focused on the words.

What kinds of people attended the performances in theatres, and then in the libraries?

Melissa   At some theatres you get quite local audiences – people who generally go to see something because they enjoy theatre, can afford it and it's their local, so they habitually check what's on. Much depends on what part of London a theatre is in. For example, we performed in East London, in Hackney, which is now a very gentrified area, with quite a lot of young middle-class white people who are regular theatre-goers. We sold out in Hackney, and it was our biggest space. Audiences in that area can afford to go to the theatre. On the other hand, at Theatre503 in the South of London, I think you've got to have something that people feel strongly attracted to or a big selling point like a famous cast or writer. That was our first venue and so, because we hadn't had any reviews at that stage, we didn't do as well there. As for the Gate Theatre in West London, I think it has a local audience, its regulars.

The audiences in the libraries were very, very small, which was disappointing. I think our smallest audience was just one person, and maybe our largest was about seventeen people. The reason for the library performances was to give people who couldn't afford to go to the theatre the opportunity to come and experience hearing the stories. But it's very difficult getting people out of their houses, attracting the people who really need to listen, or getting the women of those generations who think FGM is OK to come to watch theatre. Going to the theatre isn't part of every culture. FGM is such a complicated thing, and a lot of the people who want FGM done to young girls are the older women within these communities. FGM has been a part of their culture for so long, they've had it done to them, their mother and grandmothers also had it done, and so they think it's the right thing to do. To continue a tradition. I came to realize that the fact that the play was on for free in the library didn't necessarily mean the people who needed to hear what we had to say would come. I was naïve to think it would be so easy, especially considering my own background. When I was growing up, my parents took me to museums and on day trips, but going to the theatre wasn't a part of our life. I wasn't interested in theatre, even though I wanted to be a performer. So, what was I now expecting from communities completely distant from that tradition?

At my local library, we had several teachers in the audience, who were saying, 'Our school just isn't addressing FGM right now, the head teacher isn't interested, they're not giving us FGM training', even though it is now obligatory for schools. These teachers were asking questions like, 'What do we do, what signs do we look out for?' That was particularly rewarding – to be able to talk with teachers who came forward, who cared about their students. And that was, I think, the most interesting sort of audience we had.

And how did the theatre audiences react to the performance?

Melissa   I think audiences weren't sure what to expect. Certainly a couple of the newspaper reviewers said they had been expecting to feel slapped in the face with information, but were surprised to find that, instead, they became involved in and captured by the human drama. Isley's piece, *Sleight of Hand*, portrays five different characters in a community, and it shows how each of them turns a blind eye to what is going on. From a street cleaner to a flight attendant to a teacher, they ignore the signs that FGM is being carried out in their community on a young girl. I think the point of Isley's piece is to say to the audience, 'If you see something, if you hear something, if you think something isn't right, then please say something. Because you may be the only hope that child has.' So the audiences were able to take in these issues, and learn, as well as be swept up in the emotion of the storytelling.

Who were the FGM experts you had for the Q&A sessions after the performances? Did they come for the library performances as well?

Melissa   The two speakers we had were Leyla Hussein and Dexter Dias, who, as Alex said earlier, had also discussed FGM with the team during the rehearsal process. Leyla and Dexter have achieved great things through their activism. They did many of our post-show talks together. Unfortunately, though, Leyla had to stop at a certain point, after receiving death threats following the broadcast of *The Cruel Cut* on Channel 4. She had to withdraw from a lot of events. So I ended up doing a few of the theatre post-show talks with Dexter, and most of the post-show talks in the libraries. At my local library, when I explained that Leyla was unable to attend, one of the stewards for the evening came forward to say that she herself had had FGM done to her and she volunteered to speak about it. That was a truly inspirational talk.

What kinds of questions did audiences ask?

Melissa Common questions were: 'Why is FGM happening?'; 'Where is it happening?'; 'How can we stop it?'; and 'Is it a Muslim issue?' Many people are under the impression that FGM is a Muslim issue, but it's not. It happens a lot in Islamic countries but it's not based in Muslim beliefs. In some contexts where women cannot read, they are being mistaught by imams and other leaders that the Koran states FGM must be done, and so women go along with it. It is not in the Koran; that is a lie.

Teachers often asked: 'What do we do if we think one of our students has FGM?'; 'What if I think one of my students will have it done to them over the summer holidays?'; or 'My student suddenly no longer wishes to partake in physical education, is this a sign?' Yes, it is a sign. There were also questions like: 'How does it happen?'; 'Where does it happen in the UK – is it happening in flats and houses, is it happening in hospitals?'; and 'What are the four types of FGM?'

You later obtained some Arts Council funding for another production of the play. How did that go?

Melissa Sarah Sansom, who ran her own production company called Time Won't Wait, came to watch *Little Stitches* during its first run and we talked afterwards. Sarah invited me to work with her company, offering mentorship for me as a producer, while I re-staged the show with the aim of going on to produce a UK tour. We received Arts Council funding to stage the show at the Omnibus Theatre, Clapham (in South London), a year after the first production. It was wonderful to obtain that funding and be able to stage *Little Stitches* again, but I pulled away from a further tour because I missed acting, and because producing is a job that takes up all your time – it is a huge commitment.

Do you feel this play has made a difference?

Melissa Yes, the four pieces gave the audiences some insight, through, for example, characters who have been cut, minders of girls who have been cut and doctors who thought they were doing the right thing. I think Isley's play, *Sleight of Hand*, made a difference in helping audiences see that we all have a part to play, in every aspect of life – not just with FGM, but with anything we see going on which should not be happening – and reminding us not to look away just because something does not affect us personally.

And it certainly made a difference to all of us on the team. There were twenty-two of us – writers, actors, designers, director, producer, speakers – and we all learned a lot and found solidarity in the team effort. At the debriefing session at the end of the first run, everyone stressed how important it was to tell those stories. That might be only twenty-two people, but it is twenty-two people whose lives have been affected by the stories that are being told. Then there was everyone who helped make *Little Stitches* happen, who publicized it, talked about it and wrote about it, and there were the audiences who took time out of their lives to go to a theatre or library and watch it. Being involved in something like this is one of the main reasons we love our job.

Alex *Little Stitches* remains for me a special project because I think it captured something and amplified it, or helped feed into something that was a conversation at the time. And the types of newspapers that reviewed us really helped with that. I felt that it wasn't just some kind of jumping-on-a-bandwagon thing, but a bunch of voices or outlets or megaphones recognizing that this was an issue that needed to be broadcast and put on people's agendas and spoken about loudly. So, yes, it felt as if the play gained a cooperative, collaborative kind of attention. And it definitely introduced me to a world and a subject I was not familiar with, and encouraged me to dig deeper.

It made me think more about the question of doing something dangerous or that feels uncomfortable. Feeling awkward, trying to manoeuvre your way through uncomfortable territory, is essential, because you've got to talk about things rather than just clam up for fear of offending someone. I don't think that need has gone away from the world at all; in fact, it's gotten a bit more necessary. So, in that sense, I think the work was very important, as a personal process for me and as a collective journey for the group. I think that what we, and the plays, were trying to do is to hold difficult conversations, and delve into how each of us stands on some difficult issues that are potentially going to offend, and just seek to understand them better, and inform ourselves better. That is what I've taken away from it. And that is something I'm definitely applying now in my life.

I went into theatre wanting to stimulate change, with big ambitions about social change and behavioural change to be brought about by everyone coming together and examining what we need to examine in our society. And maybe I fell out of theatre because I became a bit disillusioned about that being effective. But I do remember, from *Little Stitches*, the number of people we talked to after the show who, like us initially, didn't have any knowledge of the subject beforehand. They said it was an eye opener; they walked out of the theatre with more knowledge and understanding and maybe more inspiration and desire to understand it further. In that small, microcosmic way, you know, even if it was only a few hundred, a thousand people, the situation is better than it was before. So, did it make a difference? There was a difference; it created differences in how people felt.

Is there anything you would like to add?

Melissa   The last thing I'd like to say is this: in 2014, when I produced *Little Stitches*, I was twenty-five. I'd never produced anything before, I just decided one day that I wanted to start a theatre company and produce something. I couldn't be more proud of the team I brought on board, where every single person did an extraordinary job. And Alex was the most hard-working, inspiring director I could have hoped for. Producing *Little Stitches* is one of the hardest things I've ever done, but it's one of the things I'm most proud of.

Interviews with the authors of *Little Stitches*

Daniela Cavallaro

Interview with Isley Lynn, author of *Sleight of Hand*

What aspect of FGM/C did you want to highlight in your play and why?

What struck me most during my research was how close to home the issue was, even when it felt worlds apart from my own life. I wanted to write something that reflected our communal responsibilities in somewhere like multicultural, melting-pot London, where it can sometimes be tricky to know where your place is to get involved, and we might not always see the whole story.

Were you given some specific parameters to work with (such as length, number of roles, gender of actors)?

The only parameter was length. While I know other playwrights set very specific requirements for their characters, I chose to embrace not knowing what breakdown the company would have and write characters who could be played by (almost) anyone, which in my opinion became one of the piece's key strengths.

What was the inspiration for your characters and plot?

Each character is based on a real person, and most of them were people in my immediate community when I lived in Finsbury Park. I'll always be grateful to them for their openness and generosity.

How did your play fit with the other three?

There was a fair amount of overlap in form between the plays, which was surprising but perhaps we should have seen it coming. After all, we were writing about something that demanded to engage the audience in a very direct way, and what resulted were plays that all pleaded with the viewer to get involved.

What do you see as the challenges of staging FGM/C-related stories?

I don't think there are any challenges specific to this issue that don't also relate to every other important story told through theatre. Or at least none that can't be overcome through an act of creative empathy.

What was, in your view, the goal of the entire performance and of your specific play?

I personally wanted those who, like me, thought that this issue didn't relate to them to wake up to the fact that protecting vulnerable women and girls relates to everyone, in every community, and we can all have a hand in ending abuse.

Interview with Raúl Quirós Molina, author of *Where Do I Start?*

What aspect of FGM/C did you want to highlight in your play and why?

The whole point of the play was to give voice to the survivors of FGM and to collect and portray people's opinions about this abuse.

Were you given some specific parameters to work with (such as length, number of roles, gender of actors)?

I was free to include up to five characters. I had to push to get my way and have a non-Caucasian actor in the main role (an FGM survivor). The argument given was that 'white women also suffer FGM'. Imagine the picture of a Caucasian woman impersonating a Black survivor. During my research I was interviewing racialized women from various but specific backgrounds. None of them was a white Anglo-Saxon; I wasn't putting a white actress in the role.

What sort of research did you do for the play?

I did lots of research in books and I interviewed nurses, international NGO workers, survivors and activists (male and female) in both Spain and the UK. One of the key findings was how some parties used this crime in a political agenda against Muslims or blamed feminism! Many of the people involved asked not to have their real names published, as this is a sensitive issue and many survivors have been threatened for speaking up. Leyla Hussein gave us one of the most insightful testimonies.

What do you see as the challenges of staging FGM/C-related stories?

It can quickly become an 'issue play' as we see so often in theatre. A play like this must avoid emotional manipulation and raise a thoughtful debate, it must be truthful and not just strongly opinionated. That is why it is so important to do your research and talk to people and put your opinions aside as much as you can. Your play, again, must speak the truth. And truth is ugly sometimes.

What was, in your view, the goal of the entire performance and of your specific play?

FGM is one of the many abuses committed under the gender-control system named patriarchy, but I did not want to hide other forms of abuse. So the play is also about integration, cultural wars, lack of support of migrant communities, patriarchal structures and poverty.

There is a video where Leyla Hussein asks people on the street to sign a petition to *protect* FGM as a cultural practice because, she explains, the government wants to penalize this 'ancestral' practice. It's all a stunt, everything is planned ahead just to see how people react to this. Picture the scene: an activist who has been mutilated asking people to sign a petition to decriminalize FGM. This is the whole point of the play; this is what one must look into: why everyone except *one* lady signed it, in a country like the UK. Leyla Hussein could not believe it. She cried her eyes out. It's not that we don't think FGM is bad, it's that we don't want to offend those communities, and therefore we 'tolerate' those practices.

Were you satisfied with the audiences' responses to Little Stitches *in general and your play in particular?*

I am satisfied with having had the honour of talking to so many people fighting against this. A playwright just puts everything together.

Interview with Bahar Brunton, author of *Dancing Feet*

What aspect of FGM/C did you want to highlight in your play and why?

When doing my research for this piece it became clear that, although FGM may be practised in part because of the interests and expectations of men, it is actually organized and performed by women. Women are doing this to other women and girls, despite having had it done themselves. I really wanted to examine this in my play, as well as emphasizing the fact that it happens in many different cultures and in many different areas. Therefore I tried to keep the location for my play as non-specific as I could.

Were you given some specific parameters to work with (such as length, number of roles, gender of actors)?

I was glad that we weren't given any guidelines to follow when writing these plays, beyond the obvious link of the subject matter. The only thing mentioned beforehand was length, as the four short plays were to be shown together, and as a whole the piece needed to have a reasonable running time.

What sort of research did you do for the play?

I spent a long time reading articles and interviews on the subject, and also went to several talks and lectures given by FGM survivors.

What was the inspiration for your characters and plot?

When writing this play, I was thinking about all the girls and young women who go through this. The voiceless ones who have died and those who are unable to speak out.

How did your play fit with the other three?

Each of the four plays was very different, but I think they all worked well together. The order they were shown in was very effective, as with each piece the focus seemed to draw in closer towards the victims/survivors of FGM.

What do you see as the challenges of staging FGM/C-related stories?

I think there will always be certain people who are put off by the idea of seeing a piece on this subject matter. They are uncertain of how visually and verbally graphic the plays will be.

What was, in your view, the goal of the entire performance and of your specific play?

Our goal was to keep people talking about this issue, in the hope that that would then contribute towards producing real change.

Were you satisfied with the audiences' responses to Little Stitches *in general and your play in particular?*

Different people reacted in different ways to each of the plays; I heard different responses from every person I spoke with after the performances. But it was great to see so many people still talking and thinking about the subject for a long time afterwards and paying more attention to things that were happening as a result of the increased public awareness about FGM.

Interview with Karis E. Halsall, author of *Mutant*

What aspect of FGM/C did you want to highlight in your play and why?

My play focuses on Safa, a young British Muslim girl, and her experience of being cut. We also meet the doctor who treats her years later. I suppose I was drawn to giving survivors a voice and recounting the abject horror of the whole process from the perspective of the individuals who underwent it. I wanted to highlight that this was happening to British girls on British soil – not that this is any worse than the practice happening anywhere else, but people here didn't seem to realize how close the practice was. In our complacency we were, and still are, failing those young women. At the time of the play, 137,000 women in the UK were living with the consequences of FGM. I wanted to look at how we recover and heal and adjust in a society that has failed us.

Were you given some specific parameters to work with (such as length, number of roles, gender of actors)?

There were parameters regarding length. But in terms of characters, we were allowed free range.

What sort of research did you do for the play?

We spoke to charities that work with survivors. Our most important resource was Leyla Hussein, an anti-FGM campaigner. She was absolutely amazing, and introduced us to other survivors, and nurses and health practitioners, so we could hear about all their personal experiences of FGM. It was really important that I did the most in-depth research possible, as I am not Muslim myself but my character Safa is, and I wanted to find a way to remain critical of the practice without vilifying religion in any way. I drew on my own personal experience of sexual assault to understand what Safa's violation felt like.

What was the inspiration for your characters and plot?

My characters in many ways were amalgamations drawn directly from survivors and medical staff who I spoke with during the process of researching the piece. I was really struck by intricate details of their stories: for example, how smells had stayed with them and could trigger a trauma response. A lot of these details are woven into my piece. In fact, one line is drawn directly from an incredible nurse we met, who works with survivors. Plotwise, I wanted us to meet a survivor as a teenager and then again as an adult, because I wanted to make a comment that when we cut girls, in many ways we steal their voices and their autonomy for life.

How did your play fit with the other three?

This is hard to answer, as I think we wrote the works separately and there wasn't really consideration beforehand of how they would fit together. We all wrote such different plays, set abroad, in the UK, or in several different spaces. I think my play focused on the survivor's voice as opposed to the wider issue.

What do you see as the challenges of staging FGM/C-related stories?

Initially, I was worried about sounding like I was preaching about the cultural practices of other communities. However, the more research I did and the more people I met who had been affected by it, the more I was convinced that this was child abuse and people needed to be educated on what was happening. I also remember Leyla talking about the hatred and bile she received from people on social media for being an anti-FGM campaigner. People would write and tell her they were going to kidnap her daughter and cut her! Leyla briefed us and warned us we might be subjected to some hatred on social media.

What was, in your view, the goal of the entire performance and of your specific play?

Exposure. Education. Understanding. Compassion. A cultural change.

Were you satisfied with the audiences' responses to Little Stitches *in general and your play in particular?*

Absolutely. I remember one survivor speaking with Leyla and me at the end of one performance. She said it was uncanny how much she saw her younger self in the Safa character. I wanted to make survivors feel seen, heard and valued, so this feedback meant a lot to me.

'Kubra'

A section of *Hurried Steps*

Dacia Maraini
Translated from Italian by Sharon Wood

'Kubra', a section of *Passi affrettati* (Hurried Steps), was first staged in English, in this translation by Sharon Wood. It was performed at the NIDA Playhouse in Sydney, on 25 and 26 November 2016, and at the New Theatre in Newtown (Sydney), on 27 November 2016, in support of the UN campaign 16 Days of Activism against Gender-Based Violence.

Cast

Olivia Brown	**Barrister**
Grant Cartwright	**Journalist**
Bodelle de Ronde	**Academic**
Emele Ugavule	**Kubra**

Director	Nicolette Kay
Production	Hurried Steps Australia – Olivia Brown in association with Nicolette Kay and New Shoes Theatre

The development of 'Kubra' was sponsored by The Arts Council of England, The British Council's Artists' International Development Fund and the City of Sydney.

The second production of *Hurried Steps* that included 'Kubra' was at the Women and War: Exodus Festival, in the Streatham Hill Theatre building in London on 3 July 2017.

Cast

Glynis Barber	**Barrister**
Teri Ann Bobb-Baxter	**Kubra**
Souad Faress	**Journalist**
Nathan Medina	**Academic**

Director	Nicolette Kay

A non-professional production of *Hurried Steps* including 'Kubra', directed by Ainsley Burdell, was staged by the Brisbane-based RedVentures Theatre Action Group at the Italian Cultural Institute (Melbourne), on 7 October 2019, and at Flinders University (Adelaide), as part of the conference Indelible (Eng.) / *Indelebile* (It.) – Representation in the Arts of (In)visible Violence Against Women and Their Resistance, on 25 October 2019.

5 Emele Ugavule as Kubra in *Hurried Steps*. NIDA Playhouse, Sydney, 25 November 2016. Photo courtesy of Geoff Sirmai, www.sirmai.com.au.

Kubra   My name is Kubra. I was born in Australia, twenty-five years ago. When I was a little girl I used to play with the other girls, we would do handstands, put our dolls down to sleep, we invented gardens with artificial lakes. I don't remember ever being in pain. My mother was always out at work, I spent the whole day with my grandmother Kamale who would give me lots of hugs and protect me with all her love. My father never played with us, he ate on his own, but he knew everything we did and his decisions were orders.

Barrister   Did you go to school in Australia, Kubra?

Kubra   Yes, madam . . . QC.

Barrister   What about your grandmother?

Kubra   No, my grandmother is illiterate. She would have liked to study, but her family wouldn't let her.

Barrister   Are women in your community not allowed to study?

Kubra   Now they are, but not when my grandmother was young.

Barrister   Go on, Kubra.

Kubra   One September morning, just before my seventh birthday, my grandmother took me by the hand and told me we were going to see a few women of the community for a little operation.

Barrister   And you didn't ask what it was for?

Kubra   Yes, I asked her, and she told me that I had to get rid of a worm from my body.

Barrister   And you believed her?

Kubra   Of course, why shouldn't I believe her? She was my beloved grandmother who has always protected me and taken care of me.

Barrister   And then?

Kubra   We took a tram, then another one, out to the suburbs where the houses were really old. We rang at the main door of a block of flats and they opened it to let us in. We started to walk up the stairs. They were dirty, the paint was peeling off. I asked my grandmother Kamale why we were going to a place that was so dirty and ugly and she told me it was just for a quick visit. They would take the worm away and then we would go back home.

Barrister   Had you ever been to that house before?

Kubra   No. What's more the toilet stank and that together with the smell of burnt mutton made a foul smell I can still remember. Everything was broken and filthy in the flat and there were three women sitting on a carpet covered with stains.

They told me to lie on the floor. Even the carpet stank of pee and burnt mutton. I didn't understand why I had to lie down. I made to leave but my grandmother told me to obey the three women. I lay down even though I didn't want to. Now take your knickers off, one of them said to me. But why? I didn't understand. Do as the old lady says, my grandmother said, and I took them off.

One of the stronger-looking women pushed my legs apart and pinned me to the floor by my ankles, and that was when I started to be afraid. I saw something glinting. It was a kind of knife with a very sharp blade, and a short and curved handle. I lifted my head up to try and get a better look at it, and straight away one of the women stretched her leg across my chest so that I couldn't see and had to lie flat. I couldn't move and I was half naked. I started to struggle to get free. I heard my grandmother say in a slightly shaky voice, 'Don't move Kubra, they only have to take the worm away and then you will be free. They won't hurt you.'

I did as she said. When I felt the knife go into my flesh the first time I started to scream. I saw my grandmother cover her face and move away so that she couldn't see. The others held me down tight while the youngest one scraped at my little girl's sex with the knife. I screamed in desperation. The pain was too awful. One of the women who was holding me down pressed her hand over my mouth, and at the same time she leaned over me and whispered, 'Imagine you are a princess in a lovely garden, you are small, you are beautiful, there are flowering trees all around you, there is a stream with scented water flowing. Can you smell the perfume of the water, soft as silk?' I shouted out that all I could smell was the stink of the toilet and burnt mutton. I got a slap for that. I shouted to my grandmother to come and free me, but she didn't move. She left me in the hands of those women I had never seen before who did what they wanted with my imprisoned body.

Barrister Why do you think your grandmother didn't help you?

Kubra I don't know. I did ask her, but only years later, when I could still feel a pain deep down in my stomach every time I urinated.

Barrister And what did she say to you?

Kubra She told me it was the tradition, for our own good, our only identity in a strange and hostile country.

Barrister Why hostile, Kubra? Australia gave you a home, gave you the chance to go to school for free, thought of you as a citizen, so why hostile?

Kubra I don't know, madam. That's what my grandmother thought.

Barrister And where was your mother in all of this?

Kubra My mother said later that she didn't know anything about it. But it isn't true because my grandmother told me that she had told her. But she didn't want to see it.

Barrister Do you think she agreed with your grandmother about it?

Kubra She must have done. She'd had to go through the same mutilation, the same as my grandmother. If she doesn't have it done a girl can't get married.

Barrister How long did the operation last?

Kubra Half an hour more or less, but time had stopped for me. It seemed to me that I was a prisoner of those rough hands for hour after hour, that sharp knife, that stink that caught you at the back of your throat. But more than anything else I felt betrayed by my grandmother. I hated her for what they were doing to me. I've never really forgiven her for it.

Barrister What did they say to you once they had finished?

Kubra Now you are a woman, they said, in the tradition of the women of your community. The one who had cut me had her hands covered in blood. She took a sheet of newspaper and cleaned between my legs. She told me to wash myself with cold water for a few days, and she gave me some leaves to chew on.

Barrister Is that it? Didn't they even give you anything antiseptic?

Kubra There was nothing in that room except the stained carpet, the silver-coloured knife and a bowl of water.

Barrister Did they make you get up as soon as they had finished?

Kubra They gave me a pad so I wouldn't get my knickers dirty. They told me to go straight home and not tell anybody what had happened in that flat. It was to be a secret for ever.

Female Academic   Kubra is twenty-five years old now. She has decided to dedicate her life to the campaign against female mutilation. Her grandmother is dead. Her mother and father have thrown her out of the house, but she hasn't let herself be put off by them. She will go on with her fight.

Barrister   The girl's grandmother has been reported to the police, but she has died in the meantime. We have also investigated the mother and the father for collusion in a barbaric act which is an assault on the integrity of the child's body.

Female Journalist   As a barrister don't you think that with these sentences the legal system is punishing innocent people who are doing nothing more than practising their noble and historic traditions?

Barrister   You are thinking in the abstract. Justice has to do with people, and in this case a young girl was unjustly subjected to a cruel and invasive operation which has made it impossible for her ever to have sexual relations without experiencing great pain.

Female Journalist   Even so, if we are truly democratic we should respect traditions. We can't impose our own habits on people who are different from us.

Barrister   They are not habits, my journalist friend, they are values, of which we should be rightly proud. The integrity of the person applies to everybody and should be safeguarded by law.

6 From left: Bodelle de Ronde, Emele Ugavule, Olivia Brown and Lex Marinos in *Hurried Steps*. NIDA Playhouse, Sydney, 25 November 2016. Photo courtesy of Geoff Sirmai, www.sirmai.com.au.

Female Journalist   The courts are overstepping the mark. They have no respect for cultures very different from their own. Each culture has its own dignity, its own truth, and we shouldn't condemn those who remain faithful to an ancient tradition.

Barrister   I suggest you ask Kubra what she thinks about that. After all, she's the one who's had to pay the price.

Female Journalist   Kubra, you should at least have some belief in the traditions of your own people.

Kubra   If the tradition of my people means that seven-year-old little girls are deprived of their sexuality with the slash of a knife, as far as I am concerned that culture is wrong and should change. For me, now, love means nothing but bodily pain. And when I have a child it will be agony, a laceration. I think the judgement is right.

Female Journalist   You are a disgrace, Kubra. You have betrayed your own community and you have put your own parents in jail!

Kubra   They were the ones to betray me, sending me to that slaughterhouse. They were merciless. I'm not asking for anybody to be punished: deep down in my heart I understand them and I forgive them, but I'm asking for justice, which is something different. I want my case to be seen as an example, so that in the future no seven-year-old little girl is forced to lie on a filthy stained carpet, pinned to the ground by the arms of women, and cut in her most intimate parts.

Interview with Dacia Maraini

Luciana d'Arcangeli
Translated by Luciana d'Arcangeli

I would like to start with a couple of general questions on the play Hurried Steps. *After the Brisbane performance in November 2018,[1] several audience members – including some experienced in political theatre – said they found it confronting, but they did not feel it inspired resistance. They simply endured it, in a way. So they wondered: was* Hurried Steps *intended as a call to arms, or not?*

My intention is to create awareness. I do not call people to arms because that is not, in my view, the role of a writer; rather, my role is to bring an issue to the fore, delve into the details, try to shed light on the hidden aspects. It is then up to individuals to decide whether to struggle – to resist, to go to war, etc. – with whatever means they choose, or not. But I insist on this point: the writer, in my view, acts primarily on people's awareness, which means getting to know and understand the issues, even when they are very serious and painful.

In *Hurried Steps* in particular, the stories are all from real-life cases, some of which I took from news reports and some from the enormous amount of material that Amnesty International put at my disposal. I had to pick just a few of the cases from that material that I found most interesting. I also made the selection with a view to reflecting the entire world, because this violence is ubiquitous, it really cuts across the whole world, although with local peculiarities. I could have picked a hundred other characters, but theatre is a practical business and you have to work within limits.

The script indicates 'MUSIC' at the start of each story. What function does music have in the play, and do you prefer that live music or recordings be used?

The function of the music is simply to separate the stories one from another. I would prefer live music; if you can put musicians in flesh and blood on the stage, that is much better, of course. However, we must bear in mind that this show is performed in schools, in city squares and in some very disadvantaged neighbourhoods. Often there is no funding at all, and then there is clearly no choice but recorded music. If you work with this kind of theatre – that is, political theatre, written to create awareness – expenses must be kept to a minimum.

So, for *Hurried Steps* there are no costumes, no sets, nothing but the music stands holding the texts to read from. I devised it to be like an oratorio. In fact, it *is* an oratorio. The actors speak facing the audience, as if they stand both inside and outside the story at the same time. They become protagonists but they also narrate stories that belong to other characters. I deemed it important that they should have this detached position, because the subject matter is so painful and intense that at times you can risk getting 'sucked under' by it.

---

1 The question refers to the second Australian production of *Hurried Steps*, by RedVentures Theatre Action Group, as part of the project that generated this book. See also the interview with Ainsley Burdell, who directed that production.

Indeed. Turning to 'Kubra' in particular: how did the addition of this story come about?

The person who urged me to write this piece on female genital mutilation (FGM) was Olivia Brown, who was responsible for the first Australian production of the play, in 2016, directed by Nicolette Kay. Olivia suggested we add a story on this issue, which is not widely known about in Australia yet very much present. Since this is a play that lends itself to adding or removing pieces – it is built like a puzzle, with fragments that can slot in with each other – I said to myself, 'Fine, let's add an issue that is important for Australia but also concerns many other parts of the world.' I felt it was interesting to address the problem of FGM in the Australian context. After all, Australia is a very advanced, civilized country, with strict laws that defend the integrity of the female body. Yet, from what I have gleaned from women's accounts, many girls are forcibly, secretly and illegally subjected to these practices in backyard operations. So Kubra's case is an example of FGM being practised by an immigrant minority in a country where it is criminalized (and the majority of the population knows little about it), while in their country of origin it is more openly accepted.

I made Kubra's story a kind of synthesis of some of the Australian cases described in the material Olivia and Nicolette sent me. There were dozens of cases, but I saw there were various similarities between the stories. For example, often the girls did not know what the adults were going to do to them, and very probably would not have accepted the procedure had they known. So there were two counts of violence being enacted: not only on their bodies but also on their agency, their will, because they were being tricked. Furthermore, I saw that in the majority of cases it was their mothers, grandmothers, aunts – obviously in agreement with their fathers – who deceived the poor unknowing children. It is terrible that it is women – family members, and fake 'nurses' or 'midwives', or 'traditional cutters' or whatever else you want to call them – who keep the practice alive and carry it out. Well, of course, they don't do it out of wickedness, they believe that in this way they are continuing a tradition, but they don't realize that in doing so they destroy the future of a girl.

I felt incredibly sad for girls who have been through this, knowing they will be harmed for the rest of their lives. A body that has endured that kind of procedure will have real problems during sexual intercourse, and in everyday life. In the case of infibulation, in particular, giving birth requires the vagina to be reopened, which entails pain and continuous risk of infection, and then it is often secretly re-infibulated afterwards, even though that practice is illegal. This is brutally cruel. Especially when you think that in their family's country of origin these girls and women would probably have found more support around them, more acceptance and care. In the country they have migrated to it becomes not only a horrible impairment but also something to hide, to be ashamed of. And therefore a humiliating and long-term form of violence.

I know that this happens in Italy too, even though it seems we do not talk about it here. When I looked for information on the practice in Italy at the time I found nothing in the widely available news and on the internet, while in Australia it was already being observed and analysed. This made me think that it was absolutely essential to include it among the array of types of violence presented in the play.

In your opinion, why is it that mothers, aunts and grandmothers continue this practice even after migrating to countries where there is no tradition to perpetuate?

I don't know. I believe that they feel somehow excluded from their original culture, and want to keep it alive with these cruel rituals. They do not realize that this is the worst way to preserve their identity. If that is why they do this, then it would be better to keep other traditions alive – ways of praying, ways of being together, ways of singing . . . There are many ways to ensure unity and continuity with their country of origin, without having the most defenceless and innocent members of their community pay the price.

I remember something that really struck me at the major international meeting on women's rights held in Beijing in 1995, with participants from all over the world.[2] It used to be always said that women's rights and freedom were the concern of only a few rich, white, Western women, while in less wealthy countries things were different and this had to be respected according to principles of cultural and historical relativism. What struck me at Beijing was that it was actually the Indian women, the Muslim women, the women from developing countries, who declared very clearly: 'We are against these traditions because they demean, humiliate and punish the female body. We think that the civil rights of all the women in the world should be based on values that respect the integrity of the female body, values that must be universal.' It was really important that they were the ones making these declarations, not the same old emancipated, rich, Western women. As far as I'm concerned, this agreement on universal values in favour of the freedom and bodily integrity of women, prevailing over relativist positions, was essential.

It is incredibly important, I repeat, that the sacredness of the female body be defended from the political and religious fanaticism that is so active and repressive of women in many totalitarian countries. Until recently, it was said over and over, even among the most emancipated women, that every country has its traditions and these need to be respected. Thankfully now we women realize that freedom has no national or cultural borders, and that even a caged bird knows that its prison is a horrific constraint. We have finally thrown out every presumption of historical and anthropological relativism and admitted that there are values of a higher order that sit above cultural and religious diversity. These are universal values that all peoples aspire to. Values that are intolerable to those who wish to keep women subjugated and docile and young people silent and obedient.

Women should fight for universal values – which, of course, are values that apply to men too. It is very important to agree that clitoridectomy cannot be justified by saying 'but that is part of their traditions'. Never. Some traditions, no matter how ancient, must be judged and rejected. This does not dispossess a people of their identity in any way. Identity can be expressed through religion, fables, myths, rites, etc., without depriving women and girls of liberties and respect.

---

2 Maraini is referring here to the Fourth World Conference on Women. See https://www.unwomen.org/en/how-we-work/intergovernmental-support/world-conferences-on-women.

In your writing there is a common thread that traces violence against women from antiquity, through myths, to the present. How has the culture of violence against women changed over time?

In Western civilization we have all been influenced by the Greek myths, which are very misogynistic. The characters who inhabited Greek mythology were often worse than humans, as they were very jealous, vindictive and evil, and often waged war on one another. Myths show us that violence against women has ancient roots: the story of Europa, kidnapped and raped by Zeus transformed into a bull, shows us that a god had the 'right' to rape all the women he wanted. And this is just one example.

Western culture, once we remove the poetic and symbolic aspects of these influential Greek myths, is imbued with violence against women. We only need to turn to the Catholic Church for a key example. When the church says that God created Adam first and then Eve from Adam's rib, and then made her responsible for their expulsion from heaven, it serves to render all women guilty of her sin. This laying of blame is an expression of the need to control women, to consider them lesser beings, to keep them subjugated, and it lasted right up until feminism came along. Sure, there were some movements in the past. Think of Olympe de Gouges, for example, who was beheaded during the French Revolution for having written a declaration of the rights of women. Or the British suffragettes who fought with great courage for the right to vote. But in general the laws governing the patriarchal family remained the same as those set by Roman Law, followed by the Napoleonic Code, and finally by the fascist Civil and Criminal Codes. I am talking specifically about Italy now, of course, and referring to family law, the law on honour killing, the laws regulating work and laws regarding violence. And the law that defined rape as an offence against public morality rather than a crime against a person. All these laws were changed only after the arrival of feminism.[3] So something has changed in this country, even if very belatedly. However, this kind of 'authorization' to use violence against women is part of our culture, of Western culture. And its roots are to be found in the very distant past.

So how can we oppose it?

We oppose it all the time. We have seen this in the MeToo movement, which is very important because of being concerned with the abuse of power, and coercion. How many women, when they apply for a job, of any type – for we have seen that it happens in all sectors, from any kind of office work to filmmaking – are told 'You want to become an actor? You want to be a star? You want this job? First you have to have sex with me.' This was the rule. And women were often silent. Now people wonder: why were they not reporting this? The answer is that if they had reported it they would have been attacked, dismissed, and in any case not believed, because a woman's word is worth less than a man's. So, what is the key thing that the MeToo women have realized? That if you are the only one to report abuse you will lose, because the abusers are powerful and they have hardened, combative lawyers on hand, who will maintain that

---

3 See the Introduction for information on these changes to Italian law.

you had consented, and that in any case you are a slut, etc. But if twenty women say the same thing, as happened with the film producer Harvey Weinstein, they can no longer claim it is all lies, or that all those women are pathological liars. This is why the MeToo movement is so significant: it teaches us that the people who have gone through the same experiences need to come together and jointly report the bully, the perpetrator. So the great strength of the MeToo movement has been to make visible and collective a personal and private experience.

It seems to me that in your work, right from the beginning, you have always been interested in going beyond a formulaic or superficial denunciation of violence by men against women. You have aimed to delve deeper, to analyse the relationship between violence and power, especially the patriarchal abuse of power. Would you like to elaborate on that?

I would say that every individual case of violence can be linked to a cultural issue. In fact, I do not believe at all in a strong gender and a weak one, one given to subjugating and the other to being subjugated. In other words, I do not think that men are by nature evil and women good, or men predators and women prey. It is culture that determines values and roles, norms and privileges. We live in a culture in which men have been given licence to be aggressive and possessive, and to hold power, to rule over a family, to decide how to spend money. All this is cultural. Over the centuries it has been internalized by women too – for example the women we spoke about earlier, the Australian ones who send their daughters for a clitoridectomy. Often women are victims of a culture that works against them, yet they do not realize this because they tie it to their origin, their identity. And they transmit it in turn to the younger generations.

Yes, and Kubra is an example of a daughter who rejects the aspects of her parents' culture that have imposed violence on her. Yet the female protagonists of your works do not often bring about a change of mentality or reversal of paradigms; instead we find many paradoxical examples of violent women. For example, Anna in Il manifesto *(The Manifesto, 1969) is a girl who has been molested but instead of being presented as a victim she is very aggressive, brash and violent herself, for reasons that become clear in the play. How do we break the vicious circle of violence perpetrated by women against other women?*[4]

Women are capable of cruelty, violence and brutality, as well as goodness and generosity, just like men. We do not have a different DNA. But there has been a long history of religious education, of psychological constraint, that has forced women to sublimate certain feelings and behaviours. Now, I think sublimation is a positive process and very important: it is the transformation of an aggressive impulse into something positive.

---

4 Violence by women against other women is present in several plays by Maraini. In addition to *Il manifesto* (Maraini 2000), see, for example, *Erzbeth Bathory* (Maraini 1991). In *Hurried Steps*, 'Kubra' is not the only story in which women abuse or kill girls. The Jordanian character Aisha reports that in her community mothers often suffocate baby girls at birth, and, in Viollca's story, Ma' keeps young teenagers captive after they have been trafficked into Italy for prostitution.

Women have been forced to do this, transforming their aggression into self-sacrifice, into care for children and older people, etc.

Statistics show women have historically been less given to committing crime, and they make up only a small minority of prison inmates. Is this because women are more imbued with goodness? No, it is firstly because they do not have power, and secondly because they are used to sublimation. When women acquire a certain amount of power they too tend to be violent. I have recently seen some appalling footage recorded by hidden cameras in an aged care home; it shows some staff, all women, violently mistreating the residents in their care. A demonstration that this is not an issue of gender but of power: anyone who holds power tends to abuse it.

For this reason it is extremely important to limit power. This is what democracy does, but something that totalitarian regimes, which justify themselves in terms of religion or nationalism, reject. For every power granted there must be a regulating authority. Democracy limits absolute power by having counterbalancing powers in various institutions: there is the police force on one side and the judicial system on the other; there is the lower house of parliament on one side and the senate on the other. There are the unions and the press. All these powers need to be independent and able to keep each other in check. But all too often it doesn't work quite like that, because those who are more powerful – be it through money, class, education or family – tend to oppress those who are less so.

Hurried Steps tells stories of violence against women and girls from all over the world. Do you think the true extent of such violence is widely understood?

I believe so; it is quite apparent. For example, the very fact that the word 'femicide' is now in common use, in Italy for example, is telling, because it reflects a widespread awareness of the problem of women being murdered because they are women. The killing of women by their intimate partners is largely a new phenomenon that owes its existence to female emancipation. Some men still believe in the privilege of possession, and do not tolerate that the woman they claim to love – I say 'claim to' because of course you do not kill out of love – should leave them. So, when she says 'I'm leaving', they are so devastated that they prefer to kill her. Do you know just how many such cases there are per year?

Yes, one every three days. For me these numbers suggest a war. We are talking about 120 per year just in Italy, then we need to add the numbers from everywhere else . . .

I agree that this is a war. Those who are carrying it out think it is a private matter, involving jealousy, love stories gone wrong, momentary madness. But when the same thing happens again and again the world over in the same way, we need to talk about a war against women's independence. Women are accessing all kinds of jobs, in every profession, and travelling the world, and some men cannot tolerate this.

One example, from not long ago: a man bludgeoned his wife to death with a hammer, in front of their daughter. That man killed his wife because she wanted to leave him, because of his jealousy – he was tormenting her. He cracked her head open with a hammer. How is this possible? And with their ten-year-old daughter watching! Yet these things continue to happen. At the time I remember saying to a friend, 'Just think if this happened the other way around. If every two or three days a man was killed by a woman. Stabbed, strangled, tossed into a garbage bin, or shot with a rifle, clubbed to death or his throat slit.' What would people say? That women are all possessed, dangerous, homicidal maniacs, who should be locked up, beaten, condemned and punished. It would be chaos, right? We need to think about it in these terms. If a woman bludgeoned her husband to death, in front of their child, just think what people would say! But in this particular case the news went practically unnoticed; there was just a paragraph in the daily crime news and that was it. All this makes me think that there is a war going on right now against the emancipation and liberation of women.

Is theatre still effective in advancing this struggle?

I think so, because theatre is the only non-virtual space left. Everything today is virtual; there's always a screen that separates us from reality. But at the theatre we meet face to face: there are spectators, an audience. They talk, they argue. And actors and audience can sense each other's emotions and state of mind. If someone wants to protest, they can. If they want to clap, they can. If they want to boo, they can. This is something very important, because not all relationships can be performed via a screen. I think the declining relevance of politics is due to the loss of a physical rapport with people. Politicians are always on screens, and so they don't engage with their audience, which becomes solely a digital metric. If you go and talk in a public square, there will always be someone who will boo or heckle or applaud you, and it is real, while on social media the thumbs-up or heart or angry face may come from a bot. You will never truly know what your audience is thinking behind a screen. These politicians no longer mingle with the people. They don't even know what's happening anymore. When there is a need to reflect on an event, or something tragic, people go to the theatre because they want to see people in the flesh, they want to see the actors' real bodies, hear their real voices and the words they speak. This is different from watching an image on a screen.

For me, theatre is the site for political struggle, more than the novel. Because theatre is immediate; a play is a text you bring to people in a different way from a novel. And it has a symbolic power that the novel does not have. When you stage something, you interpret it, and it becomes political – political in the cultural sense, of course. I love theatre very much, and I consider it the most demanding part of my work. Because some things I cannot thrash out completely in a book. And it usually takes me two years to write a novel. In that time the narrative that lies behind current events changes, it moves on. But a play can be written quickly, and so can be created in the here-and-now.

And then there's the fact that a company can tour a play easily and create a person-to-person exchange. Take *Hurried Steps*, for example: no sets, no nothing – the power lies in the words. It is still being performed today, so it's a play that is 'getting around'. As we've said, it's easy to stage and doesn't cost much at all. It only requires five actors and a coordinator, and they can be unpaid if there are no funds. The music can be recorded. So it's very simple. Not only that, but it can be performed in any language, as long as someone translates it and adapts it to the local language. It's been performed in British and American English, French, German, Dutch, Spanish, etc. So it's an adaptable text that can be performed anywhere, and when I am asked to add a story relevant to a country in which it is to be performed I do so.

So, yes, I will continue to write for the theatre. An image on screen appears to bring things closer but actually it completely distances them. If someone is killed, sure, we can see the blood run but it feels unreal. But at the theatre, even if we know full well that the blood is tomato sauce, the presence of the physical body of the actor and the power of the spoken word will prevail. Words speak to the mind, and the mind, in the end, is what raises our consciousness.

Interview with Nicolette Kay, director of the professional productions of *Hurried Steps* in the UK, and in Sydney in 2016

Claire Kennedy

You have produced and directed Hurried Steps *many times now. What drew you to this play?*

What interested me about *Hurried Steps* was the effect that it had on an audience; I saw it was a very effective tool for getting the message across. The fact that it worked, theatrically, interested me as a theatre practitioner. But I was also drawn to it because of the requirement to hold a discussion with an expert panel afterwards, and I realized that this was a powerful way of using theatre.

The other interesting thing about *Hurried Steps* is how different all the stories are. Although the style of presentation for each story is the same, the atmosphere and the flavour are completely different, and they take you to various parts of the world in the twinkling of an eye. The more I worked with this play the more I realized that, on many levels – not least the emotional level – it is incredibly powerful.

How did 'Kubra' come about, and what makes it different from the other stories in Hurried Steps*?*

The 'Kubra' story is especially significant for me as I was involved in its development, along with Olivia Brown in Sydney who spent two years researching for it. By then I had produced and directed many performances of *Hurried Steps* in the UK, at various venues, involving various types of audiences. In 2016 I obtained grants from the Arts Council of England and the British Council for research and development so that a story about this very important aspect of violence against women and girls, FGM, could be included in the play. There was increasing public attention to FGM at the time in the UK and Australia.

Olivia delved into the situation in Australia, attending conferences, meeting with people in relevant organizations including NoFGM Australia, White Ribbon Australia and Amnesty International, collecting newspaper clippings, and especially talking with women of various backgrounds who had had FGM performed on them. Together we collated all the personal stories that we could gather from these survivors. We gave this material to Dacia Maraini for writing 'Kubra'.

The grants included funds for me to go to Australia in 2016 to workshop development of Kubra's story with Olivia, who really wanted to stage that story as well, to 'get it out there'. So she produced *Hurried Steps* in Sydney, with 'Kubra' added – translated as usual by Sharon Wood – and I directed it.

FGM seems to be a subject where you 'set your stall out'. And I think Dacia Maraini *does* set her stall out with that piece: she's basically saying, 'I think this is wrong. I don't think this should happen.' The approach she chose may have to do with the source material we sent her, which included a TV discussion from the United States. The TV journalist interviewed both an anti-FGM campaigner and a woman who had had FGM done on her as a teenager, who said she felt it was an honour. I think that's possibly where the idea of the journalist posing certain questions comes from.

It strikes me that the difference between Kubra's story and the other stories is that there's a kind of normality around what happened to her, a kind of cultural normality in a community. In the other stories, what happens to the women – the violations and the deaths – is not normal. The collusion of the families in FGM is unique compared with any collusion that happens in the other stories; FGM is a very different kind of violation. And yes, the story focuses on, and exposes, a minority immigrant culture with different norms from the mainstream culture in the country it's set in, in a way that the other stories don't. Dacia Maraini confronts that head-on, in her writing, which is perhaps why some people have found it didactic. She doesn't shy away from that at all, as we can see particularly in the journalist's interview at the end.

As Ainsley Burdell discusses in her interview, for the Hurried Steps *production that she directed in Australia in 2019 with RedVentures, she decided to cut some parts of the dialogue in the 'Kubra' story. This was partly because the cast found the description that the Kubra character gives of her cutting particularly graphic and explicit, and therefore challenging. Did that kind of concern arise for you and your cast?*

The duty of care – to look after the cast – is important, from my point of view as co-producer and director. Certainly both actresses I worked with in the role of Kubra (in Sydney and then back in the UK) did struggle a bit with the text. They did find it difficult to get inside – because they had to get inside that, as actors. But not to the point that we cut any text. I think it is important to protect the performers, especially if they are non-professionals, as in the case of RedVentures. There can be more vulnerability there. But when you are a professional actor, once you have read the script and taken on the job, that is the job. The productions I've directed have all been professional, and all of us in the rehearsal room had that approach: the writer wrote this, and we are here to do this job.

If actors choose to share anything in rehearsal – to disclose personal experiences – then that is fine. But in *Hurried Steps*, interestingly, I have found that actors do not, during rehearsals. We are not there for long enough, to be quite honest; we have work to do and short rehearsal times, there is not a lot of chat, we have to get our nose to the grindstone. We do provide information about support services to our actors and there is information on our *Hurried Steps* website.[1]

What factors did you consider when casting for Hurried Steps, *and for 'Kubra' in particular?*

I first saw *Hurried Steps* in France, and noticed that the audience was multicultural but the actors were all white. I had been working with actors of various different ethnicities and I was interested to see if we could put the play on with a rainbow-coloured cast, without looking as if we were criticizing any particular race. And I found that it could be done.

---

1 https://www.hurriedsteps.org/

As far as 'Kubra' is concerned, both the actresses who played Kubra under my direction were women of colour and neither of them came from a community where FGM was practised. Early on in each production, after the first read-through, we discussed the role and I asked the actress, 'How do you feel about this, that you may be deemed to be representing this?' The actress in Australia, who was born in New Zealand, of Tokelauan and Fijian descent, was a bit worried about it, but as a professional actress she took on the role. And, in our production, we decided the character was not to represent any specific community in Australia, anyway.

Age was a consideration in the casting for 'Kubra': the Barrister was played by a white woman – an older woman, reflecting her barrister status. And, although the scene is written to have only female characters, we had to make the Journalist a man, because we did not have enough women on stage. It would have been confusing for the audience if the actress who had just spoken in the Female Academic role suddenly became the Journalist; we felt the distinction between those two characters would not have been clear enough.

Did you find 'Kubra' provoked different audience reactions from those to the other stories?

I think the audience reaction is probably the same as everyone has when they hear that information, whether in the theatre or elsewhere. Horror, and dismay. I do not find 'Kubra' more horrific than the other *Hurried Steps* stories, I think there is the same horror in all of them. That is what I noticed when I first saw *Hurried Steps*, actually. An audience of obviously disadvantaged young people trooped in, and they sat in silence. I was watching them, wondering if they were just behaving in a disciplined way because this was in France, and they did not dare look as if they were not watching because things are very disciplined there. But then, at the end of Aisha's story, when she has petrol poured over her and is set alight, suddenly all of them went 'Aagh!' and I realized they had been *completely* taken up by the story. It is the same with all audiences: there are points in each story where the audience is absolutely horrified. And so it is for Kubra's story.

At the Sydney performances the brave FGM survivors and campaigners who had shared their stories with us were deeply moved by 'Kubra' and grateful to have their experiences brought into the open. This was despite the fact that none of their personal stories was explicitly used. They confirmed that FGM is frequently carried out in unsanitary and brutal conditions, similar to those of Kubra's story, in the many different communities worldwide that practise the procedures.

You can often see the audience is deeply shocked – by *Hurried Steps* generally, not just Kubra's story – and people may feel a delayed effect too. All the questionnaires that we have ever distributed at the show have come back with utterly positive responses, and comments like, 'Everyone should see this, this should be shown more.' But it can provoke disclosures later on too; stories have trickled back to me through other people, and also some friends have revealed their own personal experiences to me, as a result of it. I spoke about this in my TEDx presentation 'Hidden Stories, Hurried Steps: Nicolette Kay at TEDxCoventGardenWomen'.[2] In publicity about *Hurried Steps* I put

---

2 Kay 2014a.

a link to that talk, and that had an unintended side effect. Schools stopped booking us to do the play, and when I pressed people to try to find out why, one woman finally said, 'Look, from your talk it is really clear that this provokes disclosure. And that one in four people experiences some kind of violence in this country. We do not have the resources to cope with that.' It definitely put the brakes on. But that is fair enough, because I do not want to create a situation whereby young people are moved to disclosure and then it goes nowhere. And there is much more material on such violence available now, especially on television.

The Hurried Steps *script indicates simply 'MUSIC' at the start of each story. What music did you use in your productions?*

Right from the start I have always used *Pieces of Africa*, by seven African composers, played by the Kronos Quartet. I have found it to be appropriate for my production. The very short excerpts I play between stories are from: 'Mai Nozipo' (Mother Nozipo) by Dumisani Maraire; 'White Man Sleeps – Movement no. 5' by Kevin Volans; and 'Tilliboyo' (Sunset) by Foday Musa Suso. I use them as a bridge between the stories, not to illustrate the story on either side. It is almost to allow a breath before the next onslaught, the next story. So, yes, the music is related to the emotional journey of the audience, but more a going away from than a going towards the specific stories.

Has your experience of producing and directing Hurried Steps *been different since you have been back in the UK, with 'Kubra' added in?*

Unfortunately, since the Sydney 2016 production, we have only done one more show here, at a festival in London in July 2017 called Women and War, whose organizer invited us and funded the performance. I have not produced *Hurried Steps* since. The climate has changed here in important ways.

First, it has become more difficult to obtain funding. *Hurried Steps* is a really difficult piece to fund, to be quite honest. It is important to me to pay the actors. I feel you cannot exploit people to stand on stage to talk about exploitation of people. And if they are professional actors and rely on this for their income, and we are using their expertise, then we must pay them. But it is expensive to employ five actors, and, although there is no need for lighting and sound equipment and technicians, there are travel-related expenses, for example. It is also important to me not to charge admission; when I produce *Hurried Steps* I always provide it for free, because then you can have everyone in the audience. At one show, for example, there was a judge at one end of a row and a group of young disadvantaged women offenders, who I subsequently worked with, at the other end. Unfortunately the young women did not stay for the discussion after the performance. For me it would have been great if they had stayed, because then they would have realized that they were sitting next to a judge, in an equal kind of situation.

In the early days of producing *Hurried Steps* my funding sources tended to be various small trust funds, and municipal councils. One trust fund that gave some money was associated with the police force in some way, and from that connection the police forces realized that our production would be useful for their training, so there were times when we had several rows of uniformed police officers in the audience!

In the couple of years leading up to my Australian trip it was becoming harder to obtain grants. We had a recession in Europe and the UK, and major cuts were made to funding of domestic violence services. So the women in charge of domestic violence units in some municipal and county councils would use *Hurried Steps* almost as their swansong. They would have a budget for a big event for Refugee Day or the 16 Days of Activism against Gender-Based Violence, for example. They would put the event on with their budget and I would obtain money from elsewhere to pay the actors so that we could provide *Hurried Steps* as part of their event. It was important to me not to take money for the production from their domestic violence budget. But then these people would retire or be made redundant because their department was shrinking. And the same thing was happening at the universities; the language departments were all being cut down. So it was an uphill struggle to get support and *Hurried Steps* became financially unviable.

There was a second type of change going on, too. When I came back to the UK from Australia and I proposed *Hurried Steps* to a high-profile feminist festival, I was told they would only be interested if we had actual victims performing it. A couple of shows had influenced this development, including, interestingly, an Australian work: *The Baulkham Hills African Ladies Troupe*.[3] In that performance, African refugees were on stage giving their own stories of abuse and escape from violence. I understand that the director had to give the actresses a lot of pastoral support, and became extremely involved with them. It is a huge thing to perform in that way, and in large theatres; those women went out on stage and bared their souls. And then there was a play put on here in the UK about stories of abuse in India, which included re-enactment of that terrible rape on a bus.[4] There was a series of women victims talking. One of these women had had petrol poured on her and been set alight, and there were other women on stage who had had various similar terrible experiences.

At the same time, I was also trying to promote *Hurried Steps* to universities for non-professional productions, so that students could perform it for the 16 Days of Activism and to raise money for local refuges. But I was vehemently criticized by a student at a feminist conference, who was saying, basically, 'How dare anybody stand on stage and represent someone who's been raped or had FGM if they haven't actually experienced it themselves?', and demanding to know if I made sure that the actresses had. Apart from any other considerations, I had to point out to her that it would possibly be a breach of employment law for me to ask that question of a professional actor. You do not ask an actor if he has murdered anybody before you employ him to play Hamlet.

I think these ideas are influenced by reality TV. Personally, I prefer to work with professional actors. Besides, the style of *Hurried Steps* does not lend itself to being performed by women who have experienced the same type of violence as their characters, because the actors have to play multiple roles.

---

3 In this 2013 play, African Australian women present four stories of abuse, trauma and survival. It was adapted into film in 2016. See https://africanladiestroupe.com/the-play/.
4 Kay is referring to the 2013 testimonial play *Nirbhaya* by Yaël Farber. See http://www.yfarber.com/nirbhaya.

Is there anything you would like to add, about producing and directing Hurried Steps?

For one of the performances in Sydney, we had a veteran feminist and social justice campaigner in the panel, and her take on the play was very interesting.[5] She was clearly upset. As she said, she had been working since the 1970s towards putting an end to this violence, and she was dismayed that, in 2016, domestic violence and cutting of young girls had still not been eliminated. After the performance she was reluctant to come up and sit on the panel, warning, 'I'm going to be controversial.' And indeed she was: she said she wondered if this play should be censored and never get performed; she stressed that there have been great strides in women's equality and she felt that this play negated that, and that perhaps negative portrayals of women should be abolished. This was food for thought, but we did not come across any survivor who agreed with her. My response to her at the time was: 'But Dacia Maraini has said exactly the same, on every panel she's sat on after the show: "I've been working to stop this happening since the 1970s but it hasn't stopped, and I just felt I needed to say something: what will make it stop?" And that's why Dacia insists on having the panel discussion afterwards: to provoke thought, to provoke discussion, to raise awareness.'

And that is why I have pursued the amateur licence route, because I felt the play needed to be shown, but it is financially unviable when paying professional actors and not charging admission. So, in consultation with Dacia, I set up the website, licensing procedure and resource kit.[6] We wanted to encourage people and groups to perform it, and hold these discussions. And so I am particularly glad that, for example, the group RedVentures has been doing so in Australia and New Zealand.

---

5 See the Introduction for comments by Eva Cox.
6 Kay 2014b.

Further reflections on 'Kubra' by Olivia Brown, producer of
***Hurried Steps* in Sydney in 2016**

What was your experience of the process that led to the story 'Kubra'?

I have shared with Niki Kay a great admiration for Dacia Maraini's work since the early 1980s when Niki cast me in her production of Maraini's *Maria Stuarda* (Mary Stuart), presented at the Ovalhouse in London.[1] I was aware of Niki's involvement with *Hurried Steps* and welcomed her suggestion that we work together to present the play in my home city, Sydney. My enthusiasm was increased by the fact that Dacia was prepared to create a new story set in Australia about the issue of FGM. At that point I was aware of FGM, but had no idea that it was carried out in Australia.

As I began to research the subject, I discovered that, indeed, none of my friends or associates knew that girls in Australia were suffering from this practice, with one exception: when I was talking with a nurse about the project she surprised me by becoming very animated on the subject. As a young woman she had married a farmer and worked for some time in the rural town of Katanning in Western Australia, where there was a Halal meatworks. There she gave medical assistance to many girls and women with injuries and infections as a result of FGM. She told me that the practice was carried out in great secrecy and that outsiders, such as herself, were not welcome in the community concerned.

Early in my research I discovered the work being carried out by doctors, nurses and social workers to assist and support women who had suffered serious consequences to their health because of FGM. This was happening particularly in Melbourne and Perth, and in major centres in rural areas with a large refugee or migrant population. It became clear that the people who were receiving this care belonged to a number of different ethnic communities, who were practising FGM very much in the same manner and for the same reasons. I read everything I could find about FGM in Australia and elsewhere in the world, and this confirmed that it is widespread and carried out within numerous ethnic and religious communities in many countries. I went on to meet a number of women who had been subjected to FGM, and many professional people who were concerned about its incidence in Australia. Attention to the problem grew when legal action was taken against members of the Dawoodi Bohra Community in Sydney, in November 2015, for genital cutting of two young girls, sisters. This was the first time a case regarding FGM was successfully prosecuted in Australia, and it gained a lot of media coverage.

Around this time I attended a conference in Sydney titled Female Genital Mutilation in Australia is Everyone's Business, organized by Paula Ferrari and the organization NoFGM Australia, based in Melbourne. From what I witnessed at the conference, it seemed that there was secrecy and denial surrounding FGM among representatives of some communities. There also appeared to be an intention to seek support and assistance from external health and social services, while maintaining control over what was seen as internal community business.

Among the many excellent speakers who addressed the conference was a young woman from the Dawoodi Bohra Community. Because of the publicity surrounding the

---

1 Maraini 1994.

court case, I initially assumed she was there to defend that community, but instead she spoke out very strongly against its practice of FGM, and against the religious leaders who promoted it. She said she expected there would be court cases in the future when women would seek reparation for the treatment they had received within that community because of the teachings of those leaders.

From meeting that young woman and others, I learned about the courage needed by an individual to speak out against the beliefs of a community, and that criticism could turn the community members inward and make them less open to change. I hoped in particular that that young woman would be able to attend our performances of *Hurried Steps* and speak on the panel afterwards, but unfortunately she was not available because of work commitments that could not be changed.

While the Dawoodi Bohra community is named specifically in the Italian version of 'Kubra', we removed its name from the English translation used for our production, with Dacia Maraini's approval. Niki and I had been struck by the wide diffusion of the practice of FGM in the world during our research – some African and Arab communities, Hispanic communities in the Americas, Christian, European, white communities – and we preferred that the Kubra character in our production should not appear to represent any particular community within Australia. I was concerned that the play could be seen, and even used, as an attack on the Dawoodi Bohra community if it remained specifically named. With early performances of any new work, many aspects are considered, and many sensitivities are observed. In this case, we sought to reveal the abuse, and the nature of it, but do no unintended harm.

What happens in each story of *Hurried Steps* is deeply disturbing, but I think that Kubra's experience is perhaps the most confronting. She is subjected to horrific abuse, then expected to accept it as having been carried out for her benefit and wellbeing. The compliance and the subsequent silence imposed upon her intensify the trauma. We see abuse of trust in many of the stories, but probably it is at its worst in Kubra's. I can understand audiences being shocked by the cruelty of FGM, but we must accept that Dacia Maraini's story about the abuse of Kubra is true in every detail.

And this is what I appreciate about *Hurried Steps*: that it employs truth and simplicity and compassion in getting its message across. At each performance, the actors, audience members and a panel of experts come together to witness the experiences and share their responses to them. I was disappointed at the difficulty in obtaining institutional funding for the Sydney production, despite the concern and activities of boards, ambassadors, associations and politicians involved in raising awareness and protecting women and girls from violence. This seemed to suggest that few people understood the immense power of theatre to raise awareness and promote change. I want to stress, however, that the generosity of spirit and support for the production from people working in the field was tremendous.

Interview with Ainsley Burdell, director of non-professional productions of *Hurried Steps* in Australia and New Zealand in 2018 and 2019

Claire Kennedy

Why did the RedVentures Theatre Action Group decide to perform Hurried Steps*? What interested you in particular about this play?*

I should explain first that our group formed specifically to perform *Hurried Steps*, it wasn't an existing amateur theatre company that chose to perform this play as part of its repertoire. We are a small group of friends, feminists, with backgrounds in theatre and community arts, and some familiarity with Dacia Maraini's work. When we were given a copy of the book *Hurried Steps* by friends in Italy, we decided to form a committee to produce it, in association with Women's House in Brisbane. Two of the six committee members work there, providing support services to women experiencing violence. We performed the play in Brisbane in November 2018, Wellington (New Zealand) in February 2019, and Melbourne and Adelaide in October 2019.

When I first read *Hurried Steps* I had a strong emotional response. I found the testimonies of continuing violence against women and abuse of our human rights on a global scale confronting. I had to put the script aside a number of times. I could only read it in small doses. How could I expect an audience to get through this in one sitting?

Yet the storytelling was compelling. Dacia Maraini's lyrical touches and warm character portrayal enabled the audience to connect with the stories and consider their wider implications. I was also interested in the style of the piece. I believe in stripping back production elements and letting the stories speak for themselves. The testimonies are told in simple, straightforward language that is delivered directly to the audience from the scripts placed on the actors' music stands.

Our first performance – to mark the International Day for the Elimination of Violence against Women – was to a large, predominantly female, educated and activist audience. As I watched them listening in spellbound silence, I realized the power of these stories to provoke indignation and ignite discussion.

In what ways was directing 'Kubra' different from directing the other stories in Hurried Steps*? Were there specific challenges?*

Initially we – the RedVentures committee and cast – were unsure whether to include 'Kubra' in our production, even though it had been written specifically for the previous Australian production, directed by Nicolette Kay in Sydney in 2016. There are now ten stories in *Hurried Steps*, and Dacia Maraini recommends that each performance include only some of these, and last at most one hour, so as to allow time for a discussion afterwards with an expert panel. So, for any production, a selection has to be made.

'Kubra' tells the story of a young girl in an immigrant community who underwent a backyard operation of female genital cutting (FGC) in the suburbs of Sydney. We knew about genital cutting, we were opposed to it, but we shied away from the violence in that particular story and its negative representation of women from certain immigrant communities within our society. So we didn't include 'Kubra' in our first production, for Brisbane and Wellington.

Following requests to include 'Kubra' in our next performance of *Hurried Steps*, one of our cast members in particular argued for its inclusion. This cast member comes from Ghana and is active in a local organization called the African Women's Network, and her desire to include 'Kubra' had grown after speaking to other women in that organization, from various countries, about FGC in African contexts, and after reading and viewing a lot of material about it.

Once we decided to include 'Kubra' in the performance, we concentrated on two themes in particular: the moral issues of altering a young woman's body without her consent in order to ensure compliance with a patriarchal form of marriage; and the dichotomy between Western feminist values and traditional values of femininity and servitude. The script addresses both these issues in volumes.

'Kubra' was particularly challenging because it is an explicit and detailed depiction of an assault on a young girl, without warning, without anaesthetic, without compassion. I found it extremely violent, in a way that the other stories managed to avoid, despite their subject matter.

In writing 'Kubra', I think Dacia Maraini faced the question of how to approach such an extreme act on stage, and addressed this in two ways. First, she set the story within a courtroom scenario, which I imagine was influenced by the origins of Kubra's story in news reports of court cases in Australia. A courtroom is in essence theatrical, and provides a context for the exposition of an argument. In this way Dacia Maraini was able to effectively express the gravity of the issue and its implications on a personal level for the character of Kubra, and on a social level for the legal professionals who argue its complexities in the second section.

The second way the script deals with the violence is by telling it in flashback, through the eyes of the adult, in the witness stand, recollecting her experience as a child. The other stories in *Hurried Steps* put us into the heart of the situation where we hear what the victim and the perpetrator are thinking and what they say to each other as the events unfold. 'Kubra' puts the audience at a distance. It's an account, rather like a newspaper clipping.

Directing 'Kubra' was challenging for me because I struggled with both the didactic nature of arguing the case, and the risk of melodrama in convincingly portraying the act of remembering such a painful event. In the second section where the Journalist argues with Kubra and the Barrister, there is no character or plot development, just the to-and-fro of arguing the different aspects of the issue: should Kubra have prosecuted her family for what they did to her; should we condemn people for practising FGC as a cultural tradition? Because this didacticism is coupled with the static oratorio style of delivering lines from the script, the cast and I had to work hard to bring this story to life. Eventually, I found that the drama could be driven by this tension between didacticism and melodrama, by the threat of the characters' emotions and passion overriding the constraints of the formal courtroom setting.

You decided to cut some text from the 'Kubra' script for the RedVentures production. Which parts did you cut, and why?

After our first readings of the script the committee and I decided we wanted to make some cuts to the text, so we asked for and obtained Dacia Maraini's approval for them. The cuts were for two reasons. First, I cut the more violent depictions of the procedure – the knife going into the girl's flesh, and her being held down by one woman while the other, younger one 'scraped at [her] little girl's sex with the knife' – because I felt the sheer assault of the act was still able to be powerfully depicted without them. There is no need for the audience to also be assaulted.

In addition, I cut some sections of the script which repeatedly described the dirty appearance and the offensive smells of the flat where the assault took place. While we – the cast and committee – understood the intention of describing these sights and smells as associations the character had with the memory of the act, we were wary of negative portrayals of immigrant women. This is a tricky issue when dealing with representations of different cultures. Our production was presented in English, and so through the eyes of the dominant culture. Non-Anglo-Saxon characters and actors become representational of something, a value set that is 'other' than mainstream culture, and the terrain becomes rocky when the only representation of a culture is violent and dirty.

What factors did you consider when casting for Hurried Steps, *and for 'Kubra' in particular?*

The cultural backgrounds of our cast members reflected the multicultural aspects of both Australian society and the global settings of the stories in the play, but were not specific to the stories. We cast around our friends and actors with whom we were acquainted, and so a Chilean man was cast as Pedro in the story of the Mexican couple, for example, and a New Zealand-born, Australian-raised Cook Island woman as the young Jordanian girl Aisha. Casting for 'Kubra' ran along these same lines. A young woman who was born in Sri Lanka and raised in France, and had migrated to Australia as an adult, played the part of Kubra. The Ghanaian actor played the Academic.

The Hurried Steps *script indicates simply 'MUSIC' at the start of each story. How did you use music in your productions? And was there any item of music associated specifically with the 'Kubra' story?*

We wanted the music to provide a feeling of hope between the stories of despair. One of the highlights of our production was the inclusion of a local community choir in each city to which we toured. The choir sang two songs during our performance – an introduction and an interval piece – both of which were chosen to express warmth and community connection and provide a balm for the audience.

We chose additional short sections of recorded music for the entr'actes between the stories, each of which reflected the country of origin of the next story. Choosing a piece of music that is recognizably Australian to introduce 'Kubra' was difficult because of our fraught relationship in Australia with concepts of nationalism and with identifying and valuing national culture – our cultural cringe. We eventually settled on a guitar piece by an Australian artist which, although not immediately recognizable to all, beautifully prefaced the loss of Kubra's innocence.

Did you find 'Kubra' provoked different audience reactions from those to the other stories?

In the post-show discussions in Melbourne and Adelaide, 'Kubra' became the most talked about of the stories. This may be partly because we chose panel members who would be able to discuss the issue if it arose, but I tend to think it is more because of the discomfort that the scene elicits in the audience. Many of the audience members at previous performances spoke of experiences they had in common with those told in the other stories and they could discuss solutions to their situations, along with the panel members. But very few of us have experience of genital cutting. 'Kubra' presents a problem that is difficult to fix. It is something that we find abhorrent and unforgivable, but is being practised by some people within some communities that are still in the process of finding their place within the wider Australian society. Interestingly, within *Hurried Steps*, Kubra is the character who feels the strongest in her resolve to prosecute her complaint in court, even though a verdict will not be able to repair the damage done to her. I attribute this to the Australian setting of the story, where women do have the power to act on their own behalf and the expectation that the law will uphold their human rights.

Do you have more performances planned, or further developments of your production?

Our production became a form of community cultural development project around issues of violence against women. The actors and choir members who were involved had different journeys to and from the production. Some had direct experience of violence in their own lives, either personally or professionally through their work in support services. Other performers knew very little about the extent of the issue and their participation in the project became an awakening. For all of us the inclusion of 'Kubra' became a learning journey, especially as a result of the input from panel members who were directly engaged in anti-FGC activism. Interest in our production grew within various women's social support services and we looked forward to further performances outside the major cities and for immigrant women's support networks, but then Covid struck. Until we're able to plan further performances of *Hurried Steps*, we're working on writing a piece on ageing.

A Trial for Rape

**From the documentary by Maria Grazia Belmonti, Anna Carini,
Rony Daopoulo, Paola De Martiis, Annabella Miscuglio and
Loredana Rotondo**

**Adapted by Renato Chiocca
Translated by Claire Kennedy
from the Italian original *Processo per stupro***

Processo per stupro (A Trial for Rape), based on the documentary of the same title by Maria Grazia Belmonti, Anna Carini, Rony Daopoulo, Paola De Martiis, Annabella Miscuglio and Loredana Rotondo, was first staged at the Teatro Eliseo in Rome, as part of the Eliseo Off programme, on 2 March 2018.

Cast

Clara Galante	**Tina Lagostena Bassi**
Francesco Lande	**Defendants**
Simona Muzzi	**Fiorella**
Enzo Provenzano	**Giorgio Zeppieri**
Tullio Sorrentino	**Judge**

Director	Renato Chiocca
Production	Teatro Eliseo

After the season in Rome (2–26 March 2018), the play was staged with the same cast at the Teatro D'Annunzio in Latina as part of the Lievito (Yeast) Festival, on 27 April 2018, and in Cagliari as part of the Pazza Idea (Crazy Idea) Festival, on 24 November 2018, to mark the International Day for the Elimination of Violence against Women.

A recording made at the Teatro D'Annunzio in Latina can be viewed on the Latina City Council Facebook page, at https://www.facebook.com/watch/?v=441694947172918.

Prologue: Video clip of the opening scene from the documentary

A female journalist is interviewing a group of people waiting outside the courthouse.

Mother of One Defendant   You know why we're talkin' to you? 'Cos he's my son, that's why. Otherwise what would I care? Eh? He didn't do anything wrong. He didn't kill that girl. He went out for a good time. She liked a good time too, or she wouldna gone with my son. He's got a wife and kid, and she knew that when she was ringin' 'im at work all the time, hassling 'im.

Journalist   If he has a wife and child, why did he go with her?

Mother of One Defendant   'Cos they all do! Is he the first? Your husband – if you've got one – you think he doesn't? You think he's gonna tell you if he does?

Passer-by (*a woman*)   All husbands do it! All of 'em . . . 'Cos it's women that . . . Women these days suck. It's us women that suck!

Many raised voices, talking over each other.

Woman from the Feminist Movement (*inaudible question*)   . . . with prostitutes? What are you saying?

Passer-by   Are you saying my husband goes with prostitutes?

Woman from the Feminist Movement   Well, I don't know, what are you saying?

Passer-by   My husband . . . If some woman goes for my husband, he's not gonna reject her! In yer dreams . . .

Second passer-by (*a woman*)   Ah, you know, with all the prostitutes round the place . . .

Passer-by   My husband's not gonna say no . . .

Second passer-by   Is he gonna come home and tell you: 'Listen, I've been with someone'?

Passer-by   No way he's gonna say, 'Listen, I've been with so-and-so . . .'. No, eh, and that's right. Sure, if I have to see it, I don't like it, do I? No way. But sure, if he gets . . . What's he gonna do, refuse? 'Hey, get lost!' You gotta be kidding. All men are like that. All men are. 'Cos if a woman . . . 'cos these days it's women that throw themselves at men . . . I see lots of 'em, I see 'em, eh, I see lots of 'em!

Mother of One Defendant   That girl, she was goin' around like that all year. More than a year. Makin' out she was goin' to work but really goin' . . . goin' with anyone and everyone . . .

Passer-by (*to Journalist*)   . . . all over the place, all over the place, it makes you sick, it makes you sick these days, Miss, or Mrs, or whatever you are.

A light goes up on the centre of the stage. **Director** *enters and stands in the shaft of light, holding some official papers.*

Director   Extract from the report filed at Rome police headquarters: 'When brought into this rapid response unit the girl reported that she had been taken to a villa in Nettuno and raped there by four individuals. She further stated that she had been taken to the villa by Rocco Vallone, on the pretext that he was going to introduce her to some people who were setting up a new company, of which she was to be the secretary. Once inside the villa she realized that Vallone intended to force himself on her, so she asked him to take her home immediately. But Vallone grabbed her, threw her on the bed, stripped off her clothes and raped her. She suddenly realized that three other men were present in the room, completely naked, and they proceeded to rape her one after another, twice each, in quick succession. She also declared that Vallone had overcome her resistance by slapping her face a number of times and threatening to kill her.'

Subsequent to this report four arrest warrants were issued, for the crimes of abduction with sexual intent and rape. At the time of arrest, the defendants freely admitted to having carried out the alleged acts. When interrogated later, they denied having had intercourse with the girl. Finally, at the preliminary hearing, they admitted to the acts but stated that there had been a prior agreement with the girl regarding payment to her of 200,000 lire.[1]

The trial takes place after eight months in custody for three of the defendants; the fourth is still at large.

The lights go up and reveal the stage set. Three tables and five chairs, and a sign above declaring 'All are equal before the law'.

Judge, **Defendant**, *and barristers* **Tina Lagostena Bassi** *and* **Giorgio Zeppieri** *enter and take up their positions.*

Director   The courtroom in Latina, near Rome, 1978.

Director *exits*.

Judge   Now let's see: the defendants are all represented by Mr Giorgio Zeppieri.

Giorgio Zeppieri *stands up, approaches* **Judge***'s table and puts an envelope down on it.*

Giorgio Zeppieri   Your Honour, the three defendants in custody hereby offer 2 million lire as reparation of damages. That money is here . . . Not to be seen as admission of any responsibility. That money is on the table. This is therefore a serious offer, a concrete offer that we make as compensation for damages, as regards . . . on the part of Vallone, Novelli and Vagnoni. These three defendants only.

Tina Lagostena Bassi *stands too and approaches* **Judge***'s table.*

Tina Lagostena Bassi   Given that the Neapolitan system of the brown envelope tossed on the table has taken on here too . . .

---

1 At the time of the trial in May and June 1978, the value of 1,000 lire was a little less than two-thirds of one pound sterling, according to historical exchange rates given at www.poundsterlinglive.com.

7 From left: Enzo Provenzano (Giorgio Zeppieri), Clara Galante (Tina Lagostena Bassi) and Tullio Sorrentino (Judge) in *Processo per stupro*. Teatro Eliseo, Rome, 2 March 2018. Photo courtesy of Federica Di Benedetto.

Judge   No, who . . .? Excuse me, you are?

Tina Lagostena Bassi   I am acting for the complainant, in her civil action as aggrieved party.[2] I was registered at the preliminary hearing.

Judge   Ma'am, your name is . . .?

Tina Lagostena Bassi   Tina Lagostena Bassi. At the Bar in Rome.

Judge   Counsel Lagostena Bassi, regarding the offer of monetary compensation . . .

Tina Lagostena Bassi   The complainant has given me the following instructions. She requests the symbolic figure of one lira as compensation for damages, because the damage done to a girl who is raped is immeasurable, and cannot be repaired with a bribe. And she requests that the amount you determine as financial penalty in sentencing be paid to the Centre Against Violence Towards Women, run by the Women's Liberation Movement and located at Women's House in Via del Governo Vecchio, Rome.

Judge   So she rejects the offer of compensation?

---

2 See the Introduction for information about some characteristics of the Italian judicial system that may be unfamiliar to non-Italian readers, including: the presence of a barrister representing the complainant; the application by organizations to be constituted as co-complainants; and the concurrent examination of complainant and defendant.

Tina Lagostena Bassi   For herself she requests one lira. As for the amount offered, we reject it anyway; we will ask for the amount to be reviewed and in any case paid to the Centre Against Violence Towards Women.

Giorgio Zeppieri   What is the justification, Your Honour? On what grounds is the offer rejected?

Tina Lagostena Bassi   We women find extremely offensive this practice, this now well-established practice, of bringing a bribe – allow me the term – a *bribe*, and placing it, or actually tossing it blithely, onto the judges' bench.

Giorgio Zeppieri   But what is the justification? Because the question will arise, I can assure you now, because it is not for reasons of . . .

Judge   She said that the damage is immeasurable.

Tina Lagostena Bassi   The damage suffered by a woman who is raped is immeasurable.

Judge   I advise the public that at the first indication of any disruption to the peaceful conduct of the hearing, I will clear the court. No expression of approval or disapproval is permitted, nor any form of prompting.

Giorgio Zeppieri   In fact these proceedings should be held *in camera*.

Judge   Well, this is not . . . the question does not arise at the moment. Whether they should . . . There is no law requiring that we proceed behind closed doors. And therefore, the question does not arise as yet. Call the complainant.

The two barristers return to sit behind their respective tables. **Fiorella** *enters very slowly. She stops in front of* **Judge**'*s table and sits down.*

Judge   Before we begin the hearing: the sum of 2 million lire has been offered, and deposited here, as compensation for damages to you. Do you consider this amount appropriate compensation for damages resulting to you from the crime?

Fiorella   No.

Judge   Are you rejecting it because you consider it insufficient, or is it a matter of principle?

Fiorella   On principle. I don't want any money.

Tina Lagostena Bassi   But she said that any fine that the court imposes is to be paid to the Women's Centre . . .

Fiorella *nods.* **Judge** *looks closely at her.*

Judge   The court will withdraw to decide on these preliminary matters.

While **Judge** *exits from behind his table,* **Fiorella** *goes over to sit next to* **Tina Lagostena Bassi** *and* **Giorgio Zeppieri** *turns to chat with* **Defendant**.

Giorgio Zeppieri   Give them a chance to let off a bit of steam, I say. It's better that way, much better! The quicker things go, the better for us. The quicker things go, the less drama, the better. For the judge the trial is already over and done with, it's done . . .

8 From left: Simona Muzzi (Fiorella) and Tullio Sorrentino (Judge) in *Processo per stupro*. Teatro Eliseo, Rome, 2 March 2018. Photo courtesy of Federica Di Benedetto.

Judge *re-enters and sits down.*

Judge   Having considered the objections raised by the defence counsel to the constitution of the complainant and others as aggrieved parties in concurrent civil actions, and having consulted the complainant's counsel and the public prosecutor, the court determines as follows. First, with respect to the prior submission by the complainant's counsel regarding damages, that the information acquired thus far is *not* such as to conclude that the amount offered by the defendants be considered consistent with total reparation of the physical and psychological injury suffered. Second, with respect to the objection to the constitution of two organizations – the Feminist Movement of Latina and the Women's Liberation Movement – as aggrieved parties, the court finds that these associations do not appear at present to have the legitimate status necessary to pursue a civil action in this criminal court. The court therefore dismisses the objection to the constitution of Fiorella[3] as aggrieved party in a civil action but declares inadmissible an additional civil action by the above-named organizations as co-complainants.

The court also takes note that the fourth defendant, Roberto Palombo, has now presented himself, in compliance with the arrest warrant issued during the investigation. The hearing shall now resume. Call the First Defendant.

---

3 Fiorella's family name was never publicized and all occurrences were erased in the documentary. In the playscript, she is referred to as simply 'Fiorella' or, occasionally, in the Judge's pronouncements, 'Fiorella—'.

Examination of Defendants and Fiorella

Defendant *gets up from behind the defence table and walks over to sit in front of* **Judge** *as* **First Defendant**.

Judge   How did you come to meet up with the others on that day, the seventh of October?

First Defendant   I happened to be at . . . in this café, the De Amicis café . . . I was there at the café playing pinball . . .

Judge   Playing pinball . . .

First Defendant   . . . when Vallone came up to me . . . and told me that Fiorella needed a loan and if I was interested in having sex with her for 50,000 lire . . .

Judge   So, your share was to be 50,000 lire. Did Vallone say the girl needed that amount urgently, that she wanted it that very evening? Is that what he led you to understand?

First Defendant   Well, he said she was prepared to come . . . to go with someone, have sex with someone for 200,000 lire. He didn't exactly say she needed the money that evening . . .

Judge   So, nobody said that specifically?

First Defendant   Not to me, he didn't say that to me . . .

Judge   And you didn't ask? I mean, suppose you go to the market to buy a radio, you know it costs a certain amount, and you go with the intention of buying it. Don't you bother to check first that, between the two of you, you've got enough money on you to cover it?

First Defendant   Well, as I said the other time, I only had 30,000 lire on me but I could get the rest from the others who had . . .

Judge   Afterwards, when you were leaving to go back to Rome, did the girl demand that money, or not?

First Defendant   Yes, she said she wanted . . . she raised it . . .

Judge   And why didn't you give her at least part of the money, at least the amount you had on you?

First Defendant   Because . . . as I said the other time . . . the sex . . . I mean, at least for me . . . wasn't satisfying . . . it wasn't worth it . . .

Judge (*to the court*)   Got that? It wasn't satisfying. Not worth even 30,000. (*To* **First Defendant**.) Why is it that . . . The girl says all four of you did it. But you, it seems, did not 'go all the way'. You, personally, did not 'go all the way', is that right? That is, you didn't have . . . complete sexual intercourse with her?

First Defendant   No . . . I mean, I didn't have complete . . . at least, I just put my penis in her mouth, that's all. I didn't have sexual intercourse . . .

Judge   I would like to know if you ejaculated, that is, if you had complete coitus or not. Do you understand what I'm asking?

First Defendant   . . . I didn't have complete intercourse . . .

Judge   But did you reach orgasm or not?

First Defendant   Yes, in the sense that . . . in that moment . . .

Judge   OK, OK, that's enough . . . Call the Second Defendant.

First Defendant *stands up, turns full circle and sits down again as* **Second Defendant**.

Judge   Now, the first question is this: you said that several times you . . . Where did you usually have sexual intercourse?

Second Defendant   In the car.

Judge   Why in the car?

Second Defendant   Because, being married . . .

Judge   Whose car was it?

Second Defendant   Mine . . .

Judge   There is no need for clarifications like 'because, being married'. In fact, precisely because of being married it would have been a good idea for you to go home . . . So, in the car, at night.

Second Defendant   At night.

Judge   How much did you pay her each time you had sexual intercourse, how much money?

Second Defendant   I took her out to dinner . . .

Judge   How much *money* did you give her?

Second Defendant   One time when we went out with Vallone, she . . .

Judge   I don't want to know about 'one time'. You said there were several times. Did you work out a price beforehand each time or not?

Second Defendant   No.

Judge   No. So, to clarify: there was no expectation, no clear agreement about payment. Just that you were taking her out to dinner?

Second Defendant   Yes, to dinner . . . to a café . . .

Judge   Every time?

Second Defendant   I remember that one time, and then that time we went to the Fungo restaurant . . .

Judge   So, you only paid for her food and drinks at a restaurant or café?

Tina Lagostena Bassi (*from her table*)   How come, if you usually had normal sexual relations, for free, or in return for a cigarette or a coffee, this one time you said you were prepared to pay 50,000 lire? For something you usually got for free.

Second Defendant   Exactly, I didn't give her that money. (*Looks to* **Giorgio Zeppieri** *for confirmation.*) Why, did I give her that money?

Judge (*chuckling*)   Ah, I see.

Second Defendant   Would I have paid her that? Is she worth 50,000 lire? Really? I don't get it . . .

Judge   Do you mean the girl is worth more than 50,000 lire?

Second Defendant   My wife's better for sure . . .

Judge   'My wife is better.' Well, then . . .

Second Defendant   Yeah!

Judge   Then you could have stayed at home with your wife, couldn't you?

Second Defendant (*interrupting*)   So she says, 'Listen, Roberto, be careful though because I haven't taken the pill.' Those were her exact words.

Judge   What did she say exactly?

Second Defendant (*articulating each syllable clearly*)   I have not taken the pill.

Judge   In front of Vallone.

Second Defendant   That's right, in front of Vallone.

Judge   And you, did you come into the room dressed or naked?

Second Defendant   Dressed.

Judge   Ah, dressed.

Second Defendant   Yeah, dressed. What? Why would I turn up naked?

Judge   And was Vallone still there while you coupled with this girl? Or did Vallone go out?

Second Defendant   He went out, I think.

Judge   'I think . . .' You do a lot of thinking here, I have to say! 'I think', 'I do', 'I say!' See if you can manage to . . .

Second Defendant   I don't exactly look around the place while I'm making love.

Judge   But we are naïve and we need to know, unfortunately we are not expert . . .

Second Defendant   Well, I'm not in the habit of . . .

Judge   Exactly. So, I put it to you: there's a woman in front of you with whom you are about to have sexual intercourse, and you see there's another man there who you think has just had sexual intercourse with her, but you don't even wait for him to leave? Did you already know Vallone?

Second Defendant   Yes . . .

Judge   Did Vallone know that you had had previous sexual relations with her?

Second Defendant   I don't know because . . . But I'm a respectable guy! You need to ask him that . . . if he . . .

Judge   So you didn't share any secrets . . .

Tina Lagostena Bassi (*from her table*)   A respectable guy . . .

Judge   We'll refrain from comment . . .

Second Defendant (*yelling, addressing* **Tina Lagostena Bassi** *and* **Fiorella**)   Is she a respectable girl, going out at 4 a.m. with two men in a car? Is she a respectable girl?

Judge   Call the Third Defendant!

Second Defendant *stands up, turns full circle and sits down again as* **Third Defendant**.

Judge   Why did you go along with them without taking any money?

Third Defendant   Who went along without any money? I had the money on me.

Judge   You had the money on you? So why did you not pay the girl?

Third Defendant   Because she didn't satisfy me.

Judge   Because she didn't satisfy you . . .

Third Defendant   She didn't satisfy me and I didn't give her the money.

Judge   Did you have sexual intercourse? (*To the audience.*) The public must refrain from any expression of approval or disapproval. (*To* **Third Defendant** *again.*) Well, did you have sexual intercourse?

Third Defendant   Yes.

Judge   How many times?

Third Defendant   Once.

Judge   The girl says twice and you say once.

Third Defendant   Yeah, well . . . (*Looking at* **Fiorella**.) The girl says a lot of things . . .

Judge   And why did she not satisfy you, in what way?

Third Defendant   Um, because . . . Basically, I didn't feel like paying her.

Judge   You didn't feel like paying her. So you didn't want the satisfaction of handing over the money?

Third Defendant   Yeah, well, I wanted to cheat her . . . I didn't want to give it to her. (**Giorgio Zeppieri** *prompts him.*) Yeah, I mean trick her, not cheat her. OK. (**Giorgio Zeppieri** *nods.*)

Tina Lagostena Bassi *stands up.*

Tina Lagostena Bassi   Do you know Mr Giaccari?

Third Defendant *does not respond.*

Judge   Giaccari, that would be Vagnoni's brother-in-law.

Tina Lagostena Bassi   So, *his* brother-in-law. His brother-in-law Giaccari. Shall we take note that he did not answer, that *we* had to tell him that Giaccari is his brother-in-law?

Judge   Vagnoni's brother-in-law. He is Vagnoni.

Tina Lagostena Bassi   I would like to ask why you went to see your brother-in-law on the second of February and why you asked him to go and offer Fiorella a million lire . . . Why? So that she would agree not to identify you?

Third Defendant   Because I've . . . Your Honour, sir, I've got a record . . .

Judge   Yes, but he's already admitted to that, Counsel.

Tina Lagostena Bassi   No, actually . . .

Third Defendant   I've got a record and I was afraid that . . .

Tina Lagostena Bassi   Given that we will call Giaccari anyway, and hear his version, well . . . Your Honour, if I may: what he says and what Giaccari said really are worlds apart.

Judge   In any case, he confirms the version that he gave . . .

Tina Lagostena Bassi   But I want to know his motives. His actions are undisputed.

Judge   Is it true that you asked . . . that you sent your brother-in-law to offer a million lire to the girl so that, when questioned, she would declare she did not recognize you?

Third Defendant   Because I . . . Because I hadn't paid the 50,000 lire I was supposed to put in, I wanted to give her a million . . .

Judge   All right, that's enough.

Third Defendant *stands up and goes back to sit next to* **Giorgio Zeppieri**. **Fiorella** *rises and walks slowly over to sit in front of* **Judge**.

Judge (*addressing* **Fiorella** *with a smile*)   Do you need moral support? There's no need, as you can see, you're not alone, you're here, we're all family men . . . So there's no need to look to your adoptive mother. (*Paternal chuckle.*) Now, when you signed the statement, did the clerk read back to you precisely what was written there?

Fiorella   I can't remember.

Judge   Then how can you now say 'I uphold the charges'?

Fiorella   With the examining magistrate . . . He read it back to me.

Judge   Ah, the examining magistrate read it back to you? Right. (*As if dictating.*) 'I uphold the charges as per my declaration submitted to the examining magistrate, who read it back to me in detail after questioning me.' (*Addressing* **Fiorella** *again.*) The question is: Vallone and Novelli both state categorically that they had had sexual intercourse with you before. What do you say to that?

Fiorella   It's not true.

Judge   'It's not true.' (*To* **Fiorella**.) But sometimes . . . (*To* **Defendant** *who is reacting angrily.*) Sit down! (*To* **Fiorella** *again.*) But sometimes you went for a drive with them in a car?

Fiorella   Well, I sometimes met him when I came out of school – we were going the same way.

Judge   Who did you meet?

Fiorella   Rocco.

Judge   Ah, Rocco Vallone.

Fiorella   Rocco Vallone. He gave me a lift and he let me drive his car.

Judge   Is it true that one of those times when you were in the car a fine was issued?

Fiorella   We were stopped by the police or the Carabinieri, but I can't remember if it was for a licence check or a fine.

Judge   What time was it?

Fiorella   I don't know.

Judge   Was it daytime or evening?

Fiorella (*looking at* **Tina Lagostena Bassi**)   Evening?

Judge   It was at night. What time was it?

Fiorella   In the evening.

Judge   It was in the evening. (*Reading the fine notice.*) Come now . . . This . . . Actually the whole lot of them ought to be charged with perjury. It was half past midnight.

Giorgio Zeppieri *makes as if to object.*

Judge   No, Counsel, it's completely correct . . .

Giorgio Zeppieri   . . . exactly, that is what we must . . .

Judge What does it matter, Counsel, if on the seventh of March she went out for a drive, even at night? Anyway, let's move on. (*To* **Fiorella**.) Go on.

Giorgio Zeppieri *makes a gesture that suggests he agrees, after all, that the matter is of no importance.*

Fiorella Vallone forced me onto the bed. I resisted and he slapped me . . .

Judge (*as if taking note*) He slapped her . . . Fine.

Fiorella Yes. And meanwhile the others came in. I mean, he pulled my clothes off forcibly and the others came in.

Judge When the others came in, had you already had intercourse with . . . what's his name? With Vallone?

Fiorella No, not yet.

Judge Nothing. Fine. And who was the first one you had intercourse with? The first of the four?

Fiorella Vallone.

Judge (*reading from* **Fiorella**'*s statement*) 'While I was on the bed they all came at me . . . At that point I stopped resisting, and submitted to his will, because he said, "Shut up or we'll kill you."'

Giorgio Zeppieri (*to* **Judge**) The young lady stated, 'They all threatened me. One, Palombo, threatened me with a big stick.' Would she now please describe for us in what manner he threatened her?

Fiorella Beforehand, they threatened to kill me, after which . . . After they had raped me, we went back into the living room, I mean, they made me follow them, and there Palombo was . . . he was pointing this stick at me, laughing and . . .

Judge How do you mean 'pointing'?

Fiorella I can't remember, but it scared me.

Judge He was holding a stick . . . A man with a stick in his hand, laughing. What further clarification of this do we need from the witness, Counsel?

Giorgio Zeppieri *mutters something unintelligible.*

Judge What more is there to say, Mr Zeppieri? Tell me.

Giorgio Zeppieri If the witness performed fellatio, on whom she performed it, and if anyone ejaculated *in ore*. If this has already been confirmed, we can proceed to discuss the testimony.

Judge Then I'll close the court for this part. Agreed? . . . Clear the court immediately. And call Vallone.

Blackout.

Concurrent examination of Fiorella and Fourth Defendant

Fiorella *and* **Fourth Defendant** *take up positions on either side of* **Judge**'s *table.*

Judge (*to* **Fourth Defendant**)   You said that you had previously had sexual relations.

Fourth Defendant   Well, the dinners . . . No, I'm talking about dinners.

Judge   Leaving aside the dinners.

Fourth Defendant   She says she never went out with me. I'm talking about . . .

Fiorella (*assertively*)   I only said I'd never been to bed with you.

Fourth Defendant   Well, for a start you did when we went to Poli, in my Fiat 128, we did it then.

Fiorella (*heatedly*)   That's not true, it's not true!

Judge   What did she do? Did she undress?

Fourth Defendant   We parked in the field there where all couples go . . . put newspaper up against the windows, got undressed and made love.

Fiorella   That's not true and you know it's not true! Look me in the eye and say that!

9 From left: Simona Muzzi (Fiorella), Tullio Sorrentino (Judge) and Francesco Lande (Defendant) in *Processo per stupro*. Teatro Eliseo, Rome, 2 March 2018. Photo courtesy of Federica Di Benedetto.

Fourth Defendant   I am lookin' you in the eye . . . And I know you're gonna ruin me . . .

Fiorella   Oh, so it's me ruinin' you? What about you? What've you done to me? Haven't you ruined me?

Fourth Defendant   You're gonna ruin me. You just wanna ruin me . . .

Judge   The court takes note of this reciprocal ruination.

Blackout.

Address by Fiorella's barrister, Tina Lagostena Bassi

Lights up. **Tina Lagostena Bassi** *stands up; the others remain seated.*

Tina Lagostena Bassi (*to* **Judge**)   Your Honour, (*to the audience*) members of the court: I believe it is important to start by explaining something: why we women are present at this trial. I mean first of all Fiorella, and then the feminists who are here in the courtroom, and me – and I am here firstly as a woman and only secondly as a barrister. What does our presence here mean? It means we demand justice. We are not asking for a harsh, exemplary sentence. We're not interested in the sentence. What we want is to see justice served in this courtroom, which is quite a different matter. What do we mean when we demand justice, *as women*? We mean that, in the courtrooms of this country, and in everything that takes place in those courtrooms, the social and cultural conception of women must change. The time has come to realize, to acknowledge, that a woman is not an object. We women have decided, and in this case Fiorella, on behalf of all of us – for this is her own independent decision, we are simply standing beside her – Fiorella has decided to demand justice. That is what we are seeking.

I won't speak for long, but unfortunately I must point out – and I apologize to my colleagues the judges of this particular court, who have treated Fiorella . . . who have treated women as women rather than objects – but I must point out that the defence team acting for the rapists here still considers women only as objects, and with the greatest contempt. I can assure you, this is the umpteenth trial I've acted in and, as

10 Clara Galante as Tina Lagostena Bassi in *Processo per stupro*. Teatro Eliseo, Rome, 2 March 2018. Photo courtesy of Federica Di Benedetto.

usual, it is the typical line of defence that I'm hearing. The defence case we're going to be presented with is already clear in broad terms. I hope I'll have the strength to hear them out – and I confess I can't always stand it. And I hope I won't have to be ashamed, as a woman, and as a lawyer, given the robes we wear in common. Because I know the right to defence is sacrosanct, inalienable, but no lawyer, none of us in the legal profession – and I'm speaking as a lawyer now – would dream of constructing a defence case for armed robbery along the same lines as they use for rape. No defence lawyer would say, in a case of four burglars breaking into a jewellery shop with violence and making off with the most valuable jewels, no lawyer would begin by suggesting to the defendants, the burglars: 'OK, tell the investigators that the jeweller has a shady past and has been involved in receiving stolen goods, tell them the jeweller is a loan shark, who exploits people, makes a lot of money and evades tax!' No, nobody would dream of mounting a defence of that kind, that just slings mud at the aggrieved party. So, I wonder why, when the object of the crime is not a handful of gold ornaments but a woman in flesh and blood, why is it considered acceptable to put the girl on trial? And this is standard practice: putting the woman on trial. The real defendant is the woman. And, if I may put it bluntly, the reason they do this is male solidarity, because only by transforming the woman into the defendant, only by putting her through this, can they ensure that women do not report rape.

I don't want to talk about Fiorella. I think it humiliates a woman if we stand up here and say, 'She is not a prostitute.' A woman has a right to be whatever she chooses, without needing to be defended. And I am not here to defend this woman Fiorella. I am here to accuse. To denounce this manner of conducting rape trials. And that's quite a different matter.

They try to sully everything. This girl, who desperately needs a job . . . And what work does she have? Cash-in-hand, unregistered. If she *was* actually walking the streets, she wouldn't need to work in Giordano's bar for only 70,000 lire a month, which is what she was earning there. Think about it: abduction and rape by four men, lasting a whole afternoon, gets valued at two million lire; Fiorella's silence, by contrast, is valued at 1 million. I pray you take that into account when assessing the amount of their offer of damages. Anyway, they offer her 1 million lire, and Fiorella, who, I repeat, is a girl who could use some extra money – but she wants to earn it honestly; even though she's paid cash-in-hand, even though she's exploited in her job, she only wants to earn money by working – Fiorella pretends to accept the offer, so as to gain time . . . I don't need to reread it all to you . . . she says, 'Let's talk about it tomorrow.' It's 7.30 next morning. At 8 o'clock there are more phone calls, by 11 she is at the police station.

Now the sergeant was very clear when he told the court: 'When I went to arrest Vallone, he was expecting it, and he said "Yes, the Fiorella business. You'll be here about the Fiorella business."' But if the 'Fiorella business' was about sex for payment, or unpaid sex, either way, but with a consenting woman, then why was he expecting the police? Then there's Part II of the story: the men are interrogated by the public prosecutor at the prison, before the defence lawyers get there to prompt them, and what do they do? They deny everything. After confirming to the arresting sergeant that they had had intercourse – because that is what they told him – they deny it to the public prosecutor. They deny it!

Who ever said a gun is needed, or slaps and punches? In medieval times they thought so, indeed, and they spoke of *vis grata puellae*, and as you'll remember that notion was still current in legal understanding only a decade ago. We're no longer tied to that idea of 'violence welcomed by the girl', violence that validated her show of modesty while overcoming it. Today, customs have changed. If a woman wants to go with a man, she does; it's much simpler. And we no longer speak of *vis grata puellae*, nor the required resistance, destined to collapse – to use another quaint expression – like the walls of Jericho.

On behalf of Fiorella, and all the women . . . and they are many, but we haven't time to discuss them . . . We want justice. And that's what I'm asking of you: justice. We are not demanding harsh sentences; that's not what we're here for. But deliver justice for Fiorella, and through your ruling you'll deliver justice for women, for all women, including – especially – those who are closest to you, and also those poor women who have the misfortune to be close to the defendants. That is the justice we demand of you.

As far as the compensation money is concerned, I've already said: one lira for Fiorella. This girl, so mercenary, who went with men for money, eh? This girl you will sling mud at, sling mud at in spades. Well, this so-very-mercenary girl wants just one lira. And she wants whatever sum the court determines as financial penalty to be paid to the Centre Against Violence Towards Women instead. So that there will be less and less of this violence. So that more and more women will have the courage to go to the law.

Tina Lagostena Bassi *returns to her seat and* **Giorgio Zeppieri** *stands*.

Address by defence barrister, Giorgio Zeppieri

Giorgio Zeppieri   I must first express a certain discomfort that I feel here, due to my scant familiarity with ideologies. No, more than that, my aversion to ideologies, a distinct aversion to Marxist ideology, Catholic ideology, all of them. I have a suspicion that ideologies – which I have no respect for at all because an ideology is nothing more than a fossilized thought; in general, those who have no ideas have an ideology – that ideologies generate . . . I won't say fanatical interpretations, but preconceived interpretations. A specific case gets mixed up with what is believed to be a general case. And now with this feminist ideology, especially . . .

I confess, we think and talk about women all the time. We're crazy about women. We've always respected them, we stand up for them on the tram. We treat them with discretion; if one of them concedes her favours in a moment of distraction we don't tell; in fact we regard them even more highly for this. We don't by any means look down on prostitution, which, in the distant past, or even quite recently, may have engaged us in moments of pleasure. What is this judgement of those who dedicate their lives to giving pleasure to others, this punitive hatred? It is the effect of an ideology. A repressive ideology that exists throughout the Mediterranean countries,

11 Enzo Provenzano as Giorgio Zeppieri in *Processo per stupro*. Teatro Eliseo, Rome, 2 March 2018. Photo courtesy of Federica Di Benedetto.

including Italy. All women are whores except my wife, my sister and my mother. This is an ideology of times gone by and now it is no longer in vogue. There was a net separation: a whore was one hundred per cent whore, a mother was one hundred per cent saint, in the likeness of the Madonna, the Virgin Mary.

Look at the concrete facts. We have here a girl who, with all due respect, because I myself even, yes gentlemen, I do not have by any means a poor opinion of prostitutes, and I know full well that civilizations superior to ours, such as Renaissance Italy, where prostitutes were called courtesans and honoured in the Renaissance Courts, and trained in the arts, where they reigned supreme, that Japan, that ancient Greece, which made them priestesses . . . I know full well, therefore, that this kind of negative view of prostitution that we have today has its origins in medieval society. This girl, who is not in a prosperous financial position, has some lover-friends. Probably it's not love; there's no falling in love. There's just the habit of pleasure, there's a friendship of the flesh, there's indulgence of feelings. This girl reacts with typically Roman 'generosity', invents her story, lays charges, and now sails into court on the feminist battleship, with all flags flying. Nothing will stop her!

The other time, when we had that other trial,[4] all these young ladies were making a 'vagina sign' (*illustrates*)[5] in the Court of Assizes. And there was no . . . What would you have done if all the men had made a sign of the . . . (*makes a phallic gesture*)?[6] There would have been uproar on all sides, for sure. But what does our charming colleague Lagostena say? I made sure it was put on record: 'The presence of women in court will have a moderating influence on the lawyers; it can sometimes constrain the lawyers to tone down their coarse language.' Because we are deemed coarse *a priori*. Worse, in fact, we commit – how did she put it, let's see, I take note of everything – as she repeated this morning: we commit 'psychological violence, verbal violence'. Verbal violence? I use Latin terms to allude to sexual organs. But a young lady here says, 'We are not just cunt', and so on. Everything is being turned upside down here: they'll rape us, gentlemen, if we're not careful.

My friends, a rape by fellatio can be interrupted by a tiny bite. The desire to continue is dispelled immediately, for anyone. So the act is clearly incompatible with a scenario of violence. It seems all four men imprudently surrendered their member into their victim's mouth, surrendered that part of a man's body that is considered delicate *par excellence*. And on which, allow me to say, the performance of oral coitus entails the application of technical skill, in a series of intentional acts, because any technical activity requires intention, volition. Oh yes, I can abandon myself to pleasure, but in this case I don't abandon myself; it is I who possess the other. And there we have it: possession was exercised by the girl, over the men. By the female over the males. She

---

4 Zeppieri is referring to the trial for the Circeo crime. See the Introduction.

5 In the 1970s, feminists in Italy and other parts of mainland Europe sometimes made a collective gesture at demonstrations, holding their hands up with thumbs and forefingers touching so as to create a shape symbolizing a vulva. The gesture conveyed claims to freedom of sexual expression and control of one's own body (Bussoni and Perna 2014).

6 This gesture is made by clenching the right fist and jerking the right forearm upwards while striking the right bicep with the flat of the left hand. It usually expresses contempt in Italy – similarly to 'giving someone the middle finger' – and is decidedly vulgar.

is the one who takes, she is the active party. They are the passive ones, defenceless, abandoned in her greedy maw.

But what does the young lady engage in with Vallone – she who is, was, his lover, his amorous friend? And she was, on that occasion, his lover and his amorous friend. She has him perform cunnilinctus on her. Her amorous friend kneels before her and kisses her tenderly, on what the divine poet Gabriele D'Annunzio – your illustrious regional compatriot, Your Honour – calls 'the second and more trembling mouth'. From which he sucks her pleasure. What, then, is cunnilinctus? It is more than love, it is sexual adoration. Its purpose is the woman's pleasure. And who performs it? A rapist? Is it a rapist who kneels, kisses, adores? Physiologically, sexually, impossible. No, it is the act of a lover. A lady who was once questioned on this point said: 'It's an act of great reverence, and implies trust in the person's physiological purity as well.' So, Vallone begins with an act of cunnilinctus, a long, mellow, evocative, penetrating cunnilinctus. The sexual activity among this group of people does not begin with a slap; it begins with the most penetrating act of love of a man for a woman. An act in which there is sexuality, adoration, and also respect. Yes, respect. There is also respect. All this is incompatible with rape. What is rape? Violence, the opposite of sexuality. An insane and demonic desire to crush a fellow human being . . . humiliate, mortify . . . There's hardly ever desire, hardly ever pleasure. Mention has been made of the Circeo trial, which we acted in not long ago, regarding events that took place in a villa not far from here. What did we discover, in that case? That was very clearly a case of sexual violence; I am a defence barrister but I admitted that at the time and I admit it again now. That was about impotence, my friends. The rapists' impotence.

Giorgio Zeppieri *returns to his seat and* **Tina Lagostena Bassi** *stands up.*

Reply by Fiorella's barrister

Tina Lagostena Bassi   Actually, what has transpired in this court speaks for itself. And it is the reason why thousands of women do not report rape, why they do not go to the law. Two things led me to take on this case: concern for Fiorella's rights to be respected, and something else which, I have to admit, has nothing to do with this trial: I read recently in the late edition of the newspaper *Paese Sera* about another episode of violence, perpetrated on a seventeen-year-old girl – who won't tell any lies about it because she's deaf and mute. She was very, very badly beaten, because it seems she put up the kind of resistance that the defence here insists there should have been from Fiorella. I wonder what the reaction would have been. There were four men. Sure, you can bite and risk your life – and she would indeed have risked her life. Every woman knows what has happened to those who've tried to fight back, what happens to those who resist rape. This is why we say there *is* violence, violence is present, even when there is no resistance of that kind. Because not all women can be expected to prefer death to submission, like Saint Maria Goretti the virgin martyr.

This is not a matter of one person's word against another's. What we have here is a matter of taking advantage of a girl, of a girl's good faith. She went along with Vallone trustingly, because she knew him, because until then she'd only had normal relations with him, nothing sexual, because she knew Vallone was married, because in her eyes he was an older man, not someone to think of in that way, a man with a wife . . .

I will finish here. I entrust the cause of justice to you, also on behalf of that other girl who has no voice to demand it.

Blackout.

Second video clip from the documentary

A female journalist is trying to interview the defendants, who are seated in a row in court, chewing gum.

Fourth Defendant   I've got nothin' to say. She's just ruined us, that's all. Just wants to ruin us, that's all. Now the trial's on we can say it. I've got no idea what's behind this whole business.

Journalist   It's been eight months?

Fourth Defendant   Eight months we've been in jail.

Journalist   But you would have been expecting something like this. Weren't you expecting it? Have you discussed it together, or not? (*The defendants' gestures indicate indifference and denial.*) So you haven't talked about it at all. Have your wives come to visit you in jail over the eight months, or not? Haven't they ever come to visit you? (*The defendants make further gestures of denial.*) I don't believe it. I'll write it, but if it's not true they're going to look pretty bad. (*Turns to another defendant.*) Have your wives come to visit you? Have you had visits from your wives? (*The defendant gives a small nod.*) Ah, so they have . . . Have they or not?

Third Defendant   We've already had a hard enough time here . . .

Journalist   Sure, but that's not my fault!

Third Defendant   There's no point hassling us with this stuff. Leave us alone . . .

Journalist   OK. I just wanted to hear the truth from your point of view . . .

Third Defendant   Well, you're about to hear the truth.

Reading of the verdict and sentencing

Lights up. All stand.

Judge   This court, on behalf of the Italian people, with reference to articles 483, 488 and 489 of the Criminal Code, declares the defendants Rocco Vallone, Cesare Novelli, Roberto Palombo and Claudio Vagnoni guilty as charged, with general mitigating circumstances to be taken into account for all four, as well as the specific mitigating circumstance for Vallone, Vagnoni and Novelli in relation to their offer of compensation. The court declares the sum of two million lire offered as compensation for damages to be appropriate, and directs that this sum be awarded to the complainant, Fiorella —. The court further determines that consideration of the mitigating circumstances outweighs consideration of Novelli's recidivism. The court sentences Rocco Vallone, Cesare Novelli and Claudio Vagnoni each to one year and eight months imprisonment, and Palombo to two years and four months imprisonment, in addition to payment of the compensation money to the complainant, Fiorella —, plus payment of her costs of 435,000 lire, of which lawyers' fees make up 300,000, and the trial costs. The court grants Rocco Vallone, Cesare Novelli, Roberto Palombo and Claudio Vagnoni parole and orders their immediate release from custody unless detained for other reasons. The hearing is closed.

Blackout.

Director   In 1978 the Criminal Code still classified rape among 'crimes against public morality and decency', which explains the very light sentences in this case. It was only in 1996, after a long political struggle, that the Criminal Code was changed to classify rape among 'crimes against a person's freedom', with much harsher sentences for those convicted, and therefore changed to consider a woman a person. Only in 1996.

Interview with Renato Chiocca

Daniela Cavallaro
Translated by Claire Kennedy

How did this play come about?

I first saw the documentary *Processo per stupro* in the summer of 2016, following a festival of films by women directors organized in Latina by the Lilith Women's Centre, which provides support services and runs a refuge for women experiencing violence. One of the creators of *Processo per stupro*, Loredana Rotondo, was a member of the jury for the festival competition. So I decided to investigate. I already knew that the documentary had been shot in Latina, and the fact that Loredana Rotondo was returning to the city piqued my interest. I discovered that the film was available in full on YouTube, although without proper authorization. So I watched it, and was struck right from the start by the tension evident in the trial. But on hearing the closing speeches in court by the barristers Tina Lagostena Bassi and Giorgio Zeppieri, I was particularly struck by the power of their words – and their current relevance, because they called to mind discussions that are on the media's agenda today. I thought it would be interesting to listen to those words again, detached from the documentary and its precise historical setting, to explore the effect they might have in a different medium, in a different art form. So I thought of the theatre, because, as well as evoking a scene in a space, theatre – at least a certain type of theatre – seeks out the potency of words. I felt that those words, originally spoken in real life, then recorded and related through the documentary film, could be brought to life again in theatre.

To obtain the documentary makers' permission for my adaptation, I decided to consult Loredana Rotondo first and raise the idea with her. But before I actually spoke with her, she sent me a photocopy of the transcript – which is in a book published by Einaudi in 1980, now out of print; a very important document.[1] The book doesn't contain the entire court proceedings, which took place over two days, just the parts included in the one-hour documentary. This alone makes you realize the considerable dramaturgical work carried out by the directors. Reading the transcript, detached from the film, confirmed my view of the intrinsic power of those words. Then the following year I had the opportunity to embark on production of the play, thanks to the Teatro Eliseo in Rome, and it was at that point that I spoke to Loredana Rotondo, because there was a real possibility of carrying out my project.

In 2017 Federica Miraglia was planning the Eliseo's first Off programme, a season of innovative productions to flank the programming of the Eliseo itself and its smaller theatre, the Piccolo Eliseo. I saw this as my opportunity, because I thought that a project that took as its starting point the words of a documentary, and that tackled such an important topic, might attract their interest. So I made the proposal, setting out briefly what I aimed to do – 're-stage' in a theatre what had been 'staged' in a criminal court forty years earlier – and explaining that the play would draw faithfully on the transcript

---

1 Belmonti et al. 1980.

of the documentary. It's important to acknowledge here the open-mindedness and foresight of the people involved in Eliseo Off, who put their faith in the project on the basis of a mere outline, set out in just a few pages. This is not something that can be taken for granted; in Italy it's not easy to get a production off the ground.

While remaining faithful to the text of the documentary, what changes did you make for the theatrical staging?

The adaptation called for considerable thought about the words of the text, because a documentary describes reality, while theatre must evoke it.

So, in my adaptation of the documentary transcript into a playscript some cuts were necessary, but I maintained the textual integrity of the segments chosen for inclusion. That's why I use the word 'faithful' for my adaptation. The process was driven above all by my intention to create a dichotomy, a net contrast between the two sides, which I believed would make for greater theatrical impact. So, instead of having four defence barristers for the four defendants, I chose to incarnate the defence in a single barrister, Giorgio Zeppieri. He was the most important of the four at the time and the one whose closing arguments have gone down in history. So the first change I made was to cut the main speeches by the other defence barristers and attribute their occasional questions and interjections to Zeppieri. I also cut the public prosecutor's lines, which might have weighed the performance down with legal detail. Lastly, I cut the testimony of the witnesses – the arresting policeman and Fiorella's mother – each of whom appears in only one short dialogue in the film.

I felt that these cuts, made in the interests of dramaturgical economy, would not compromise audience understanding of the trial; rather, they would serve to highlight its universal elements. Aside from these cuts, the words spoken on stage were exactly the words that had been captured in the documentary.

I included two 'asides' delivered by the director. In the first, just before the actors come on stage, the words are exactly those spoken in voiceover near the start of the documentary, summarizing the events leading up to the trial. The second, which concludes the performance, is an added statement in which I highlight the relatively light sentences and the significance of this trial and the documentary in the process towards the law reform of 1996, which audiences may not always be familiar with.

Two excerpts from the documentary are screened within the play. Why did you include those?

I decided to insert clips of the two scenes in the documentary that are not part of the trial proper. The first is the excerpt that introduces the context outside the court building, through the voices of the defendants' mothers. By opening the play in the same way as the documentary, I wanted to describe the atmosphere of that moment, around the trial, but also, most importantly, to openly 'declare' the documentary as the source of the play. In no way did I want to appropriate to myself the very valuable work of documentation, of bearing witness, that had been carried out by the filmmakers. At the same time, this insertion served to establish a separation: the trial itself became theatre and everything that was not part of the trial proper was declared as such through the use of clips from the documentary.

The second excerpt is the journalist's interview of the four defendants just before the start of proceedings. Although it takes place inside the courtroom, it is again distinct from the trial proper. I shifted it from its position quite early in the documentary and placed it towards the end of the play, between the barristers' closing arguments and the Judge's reading of the verdict and sentence. There were three main reasons for these decisions. The first is that, dramaturgically speaking, the insertion of only one excerpt would not have been very logical, or satisfying, but by adding the second I could create an internal 'rhyme' while declaring the play's origin in real life. The second reason has to do with my decision to have a single actor play all four Defendants. Placing the interview excerpt just before the Judge's ruling, and making the switch from stage to screen at that moment, helped remind the audience that the four Defendants were real people (although their names are unimportant and are not given in that excerpt), and that all the words in the play had originally been uttered by real people. The third reason was to have some passage of time between the end of the barristers' speeches and the Judge's verdict. That gap in time could have been implied through a simple change of lighting, but by positioning that fragment of video in that moment I could increase the tension by delaying the outcome, that is, by delaying the response to the demand for justice that, at this point, is felt by the audience too.

How did the particular space you had for the Teatro Eliseo performances influence your directorial choices and your work with the actors?

The space we used was normally the foyer area for the second balcony of the main theatre, and had a rectangular layout, like a plain room. There was space for only twenty-five seats. Rather than create a net separation between audience and stage, I decided to take full advantage of the potential the space offered, by configuring practically the whole room as the set. I placed the two barristers' tables at one end and the Judge's table at the other, with two chairs in front of it to be used for the examination of Fiorella and the Defendants. The doors to the balcony were in the wall behind the Judge, and this made it easy for him to exit to prepare the ruling. Above those balcony doors we hung a sign saying 'All are equal before the law' – this was the only set element apart from the tables and chairs. Within the completely black setting we hung a white cloth behind the barristers' tables, covering the full width of the wall, on which to project the documentary excerpts. The audience was spread along the long sides of the rectangle, so as to leave the central part of the space completely free for the actors; this area provided the path to the Judge's bench and, most importantly, a real forum area for the barristers' speeches.

The benefit was that the audience, arranged on the two sides, could create a kind of montage of the action for themselves, by turning their heads from side to side like the spectators at a tennis match. They were free to let their gaze wander as they chose, through 180 degrees of theatrical space inhabited by the actors. So, in effect, I forced the audience members to keep turning their heads, but at the same time I gave them the freedom to watch everything that happened on the set at any time. Most importantly, they were able to look the barristers in the eye during their speeches. Indeed, a specific direction I gave the actors playing the barristers was to speak directly to the audience, as if they were addressing the jury in a courtroom in the United States. So this was actually another change made in the shift from documentary to stage, but it was a minor infidelity that was effective theatrically, in that it gave even greater weight to the words.

This approach required the actors to be constantly engaged in performance: nobody but the Judge ever exited the scene. The very close proximity of the audience required the actors to maintain a high level of tension, which the audience was also then drawn into. So there was an exchange of energy between actors and audience that brought remarkable emotional authenticity to what was happening in the play – so much so that at times audience members were visibly moved, caught up by strong emotions.

How did you choose the actors?

In the casting I was definitely influenced to some extent by the impressions conveyed by the documentary. I don't mean in terms of appearance – I wasn't interested in outward resemblance to the real people – but in terms of evoking the emotions and personality of the individual characters.

For the part of Tina Lagostena Bassi I chose Clara Galante, who trained at the Silvio d'Amico National Academy of Dramatic Art and has extensive acting experience in significant works of Italian and European theatre. But an important factor in this choice was the artistic direction that she has taken in her work: she has herself created plays on women's issues. So I thought her personality was in tune with the character of Tina Lagostena Bassi, who was not just a barrister but a barrister with a commitment to civil rights. It's as if Clara Galante in theatre and Tina Lagostena Bassi in legal practice were somehow in harmony, well matched in their engagement with social issues. This meant that, in addition to having the necessary theatrical skill and artistic persona, Clara Galante brought a commitment to the role that was quite fundamental.

Enzo Provenzano has a great deal of experience, a powerful stage presence, and a physicality that conferred a certain social authority on the character Zeppieri, coupled with the voice of a great orator. So he gave Zeppieri the necessary air of a professional man, an air of respectability, which was to be subverted by his own words as the play progressed.

The Judge was played by Tullio Sorrentino, who also trained at the Silvio d'Amico Academy. He too has extensive theatrical experience, and a solid career in cinema, theatre and television. I chose him for an important reason: his gravelly voice. He is from Naples originally, while the real judge, Colaiuta, was from Abruzzo. The vaguely southern accent Tullio Sorrentino can adopt allowed him to convey a certain southern-male familiarity combined with the authority of a judge. So I chose him because his portrayal of the Judge could be delivered in a voice that was not that of an objective, rational court concerned only with the law, but that of a court with a human face – something that Colaiuta always represented.

For the role of the Defendants I chose Francesco Lande: one actor to portray four characters – a challenge both in the staging and the acting. Here too I had a specific motive: Francesco Lande had created a play called *Chi resiste nella palude* (Holding Out on the Marshland) which tells stories of his family who lived in the Pontine Marshes.[2] In that work, which he also wrote and directed, he played various characters

---

2 The Pontine Marshes is an area of once swampy and malaria-infested land near the coast south of Rome. In the 1930s Mussolini's regime forcibly removed the sparse existing population and brought in thousands of workers to dig canals, prepare the land for agriculture and build infrastructure. Latina, where *Processo per stupro* is set, was created by Mussolini in 1932 as one of several new towns on reclaimed land, and initially called Littoria.

with different voices, and created changes of scene by using just his body, sometimes with only tiny movements. Such is the array of creative resources and tools of expression that he has at his disposal. In addition, I have always thought of Francesco Lande as an actor with a particularly reassuring presence, a presence that can have an immediate appeal for an audience – appeal that in this case was to be undermined by his words as the trial unfolded, similarly to the barrister Zeppieri. In sum, in the choice of these actors I was not always guided by their personality, but sometimes the opposite, and this was in part due to my intention to challenge common assumptions about behaviours that can lead to violence.

Fiorella was played by Simona Muzzi, whose development as an actor I have observed first hand, as she was a student of mine. I am impressed by the way she has developed her own skills of expression. In the role of Fiorella she was able to use her natural fragility but without being subordinate to it; on the contrary, she brought emotions into play on the set in a controlled way, with awareness and stage presence. Being young and only in the early stage of her career, she could act with a different rhythm from the others. This helped us in the characterization of Fiorella: a different pace, a different rhythm. While the other characters inhabit the scene with a more forceful presence – whether out of aggressiveness, or competence, or force of habit, whether using rhetoric, or eloquence, or even vulgarity – the character Fiorella appears completely ill-prepared in that context. In real life, Fiorella decided to report the crime and press charges, courageously facing up to first the judicial process and then the media circus after the documentary was televised. It was important to convey that determination as well as her emotional vulnerability. In my view, that emotional vulnerability itself tells of Fiorella's strength, the strength to face up to her own fears, even – or perhaps especially – in court.

With one actor portraying all four Defendants, what did you and Francesco Lande do to ensure the public realized they were four different men?

First there was the expedient of inserting announcements by the Judge: 'Call the First Defendant', 'Call the Second Defendant' and so on. These minimal insertions served to remove any ambiguity, because, as each Defendant was called, the audience expected to see a different character. I asked Francesco Lande to react to each of these announcements by standing up and making a 360-degree turn, so that the audience stopped looking his character in the eye and momentarily lost sight of him, and then, on seeing him again, found him changed. Clearly, there was also a different characterization of each of the four – they had different ways of speaking, sitting, gesturing and looking at the other characters. And, of course, each had his own words. These three elements allowed a pact to be made with the audience members, for them to believe they were watching four different characters.

The idea was to detach the characters from the identity of the real people involved. And in fact this holds for the whole play: it does not focus on the names of the Defendants, it focuses on the behaviour of those individuals in the particular context of a particular event. We're not on a quest to discover the identity of the culprit; this is a tale of the administration of justice. So the integration of the four men's attitudes and actions into the performance of a single actor allowed us to universalize their behaviour. And here lies one of the challenges of this play: to detach ourselves from the historical reality of the film, to abstract the words from it in order to reveal their universal value, independent of the identity of the actual individuals involved.

So did you use the documentary at all in your work with the actors?

I showed them the documentary right at the start, in order to convey the importance of the project and explain where it came from. After that I chose to detach us completely from the documentary. After all the adaptations and changes I'd made, I wanted everyone to take the playscript as our starting point, so as to seek out a new interpretation and construct new characters. So, the actors and I began with a focus on their characters' words, looking for new motivations for those words to be expressed – new with respect to the documentary, that is.

What was your approach to the costumes and set design?

As I've mentioned, the choice of characters reflected my intention to create a dichotomy. The visual impact of the set was also important in this respect, so we used just two colours: black and white. All the furniture was black – the tables and chairs – and the setting was all black except for the white screen behind the barristers. The only elements that suggested a courtroom, apart from the 'All are equal before the law' sign, were the Judge's and the barristers' robes, but such a robe is enough to transform a theatre immediately into a courtroom. The robes being black, we chose an alternation of black and white for the rest of the costumes: generally black on the outside and white underneath – the bright, luminous core inside every person. So that meant black robes on top for the Judge and barristers, and a black leather jacket for the Defendants so as to suggest a streetwise character, with a white shirt underneath for all of them. Fiorella was the only character without an outer garment: she wore just black pants and a white shirt – as if exposed, in a way – in order to distinguish her from the others.

So the black and white theme guided the choice of costumes and set elements, which were minimal, essential, purely functional to the action. Furthermore, it was suggestive of the black and white of the documentary and also helped ensure the two documentary excerpts inserted into the play did not appear too jarring.

What about the lighting?

My lighting design was concerned primarily with highlighting the action. There were no special effects, but simply the illumination of the characters in action (by 'action' I mean to include when they were listening, of course) with a colour temperature that was quite cool. I mean, this was the case during the first half of the trial proceedings, when there was interaction between the characters – apart from the short direct exchange between Fiorella and one Defendant, during which we excluded the barristers, and at the end of which we went to blackout, as if to mark out a change of scene. In the 'asides' with me on stage, and during the barristers' speeches, we turned off the lights on the other characters, concentrating on the speaker, whose delivery was aimed beyond the fourth wall. Similarly, during the reading of the verdict and sentence we only lit the Judge, keeping all the other characters backlit, with the Judge's speech directed at the audience.

After the sixteen Eliseo Off shows in March 2018, you performed the play in Latina in April and Cagliari in November. How did the staging change in Latina and Cagliari?

The success at the Eliseo encouraged us to propose the play to other venues. The idea of performing it in Latina was central, of course, especially as we realized that transferring the words of the trial from that city's courtroom to its theatre was likely to be something of a provocation. We saw the theatrical experience as potentially offering a way for the people of the city to hear and respond to the words of the trial once again, and in a different way – in a way that was informed by awareness of the city's history. Perhaps a way of re-processing the trial.

The Teatro D'Annunzio in Latina had a capacity of 500 at the time. This mass of spectators, filling the stalls and the balcony, meant we had to rethink the staging completely, especially because we had to work in a traditional theatre structure, with a net separation between stalls, balcony and stage. So, in Latina the set faced the audience – an arrangement that was more similar to that of a real courtroom, in which the members of the public are positioned behind the witnesses being examined but facing the judges. To allow full visibility, we placed the Judge's bench at the centre, with a chair on each side for Fiorella and the Defendants during their examination, and the tables of the two barristers further out to the sides. Above the Judge's desk we hung a screen in mid-air, which was used for projecting both the excerpts of the documentary and the black and white sign 'All are equal before the law'.

Another element that made the Latina set-up more similar to a real court environment was the use of microphones. These were fixed on the barristers' and the Judge's tables, and set on stands in front of the chairs for the examination of Fiorella and the Defendants. The microphones allowed the words to reach 500 audience members without the actors having to project their voices in a way that would have changed their performance and made it more theatrical. So we were able to maintain a fairly realistic voice register, and bring in some body movements and positions in relation to the microphones that are commonly used in a trial setting.

Naturally, the barristers' speeches were delivered in front of the proscenium. The lighting effects were designed similarly to those of the Eliseo, to increase or decrease attention to certain areas of the stage.

Although the actors performed the roles in a similar way as far as possible, the change from the 'chamber-play' setting at the Eliseo to that of the traditional theatre at the D'Annunzio, and the amplification of their voices, made for a significant difference in the outcome. At the Eliseo the tension due to proximity meant that the play could be experienced by both the actors and the spectators with a kind of unfiltered authenticity, with a tension that constantly held the spectators' gaze. But in the bigger setting of the D'Annunzio, the play became more of a civic experience, less intimate and empathetic, more public: the theatre returned to its civic function of *agora*, site of public debate. The words were no longer delivered and received on an individual scale; they were words that echoed in a vast theatre, thundering with importance and immediacy. So I see the two experiences, in Rome and Latina, as complementary.

In Cagliari the staging was similar to that in Latina, for an audience of approximately 250 people.

Do you know if the people who came to the play had already seen the documentary?

In all the publicity material – for the Eliseo Off season in Rome, and for the subsequent performances at the Lievito Festival in Latina and the Pazza Idea Festival in Cagliari – it was clearly stated that the play came from the documentary. But the documentary was forty years old by then, and had not been shown again on television in that time. The audiences were on average too young to have a memory of its screening. It's true that it's available on YouTube, but only people who know to look for it will have seen it there. So most spectators were discovering the documentary only through the play.

In Latina, there were definitely some people in the audience who had not only seen the documentary but had been present at the trial in 1978. The Lilith Women's Centre, which contributed to promotion of the play and its sponsorship within the Lievito Festival in Latina, was a product of the feminist movements of the 1970s, and some of its founding members had been in the courtroom. But I think that still only a minority among the audience was familiar with the documentary, because there were 500 people, of all ages, including school students.

Were there students at the Rome performances too?

Yes. As part of its Eliseo Off season, the theatre had set up agreements with various secondary schools in Rome, so that students could come to see plays and meet their creators beforehand.

For these sessions with students, the actors came too, to explain the work we'd done together taking the documentary (which we showed them) as starting point. We talked with the students about the process – the analysis and the thinking behind the creation of a play of this kind, which is based on reality but can draw from that reality the spark for new thoughts and ways of thinking. And obviously we explained the evolution of the law in the interim, especially the 1996 law that redefined rape as no longer a crime against public morality but against a person.

The students who came to these meetings of an afternoon before seeing the play in the evening were among the most attentive audience members. And they seemed surprised at what the adaptation had produced, partly because they had met the cast members and they hadn't expected to hear those people speak those words. I have to say that I observed the play to be making a stronger impression on the students than the documentary.

What impact did the play have on the audiences in general, both in the more intimate setting of the Eliseo Off and in the traditional setting in Latina and Cagliari?

Unlike film, theatre forces you to inhabit the same space as the actors, and to hear words spoken live, in a physically shared space and time. That's what theatre is.

I felt the audience was always taken by surprise at the power of those words. At every performance they repaid us with a tremendous silence, a palpable tension. Both in Rome and Cagliari I personally witnessed some spectators, men and women, being deeply moved. Some women were moved to tears.

In Latina I think there was also a kind of discovery of a dark heart – like a discovery of something from your past that's murky, and encountering it again means you have to reckon with it.

What do you feel were the implications of your being a man creating this play, based on a documentary created by women? In what way do you think your own world view influenced the play?

I didn't approach the play consciously as a 'male author', but as a human being. I interpret violence against women as a violation of human rights. After all, for me it's an established fact that rape is violence against a person, whether man or woman. I don't know how much this may have influenced audience interpretations. The point is that I tried as far as possible to universalize the problem. And then, of course, those words speak for themselves.

I must add that Loredana Rotondo was the first to ask me the question: how come a man, today, chooses to carry out this project? And I answered her in the same way. She came to one of the first performances in Rome, along with some women from the Lilith Women's Centre. I have to say she was pleasantly struck by the transformation that the words had undergone – those words that had been such an important part of her life.

However, she saw a fragility in the characterization of Fiorella that did not match up with the real Fiorella that she knew. But theatre allows us to live day by day, or evening by evening, and improve what we do; it's not like film, where once the image is printed it remains fixed. Simona Muzzi and I tried to take on board this observation, while recognizing that it reflected Loredana Rotondo's particular perspective, and apply it in the evolution of Simona's performance over the subsequent shows, yet without completely sacrificing that fragility of hers. Instead we sought to wed that fragility, that sensitivity, to the courage and strength Fiorella showed in her demand for justice and her legal and social struggle. I don't believe that in order to struggle you have to put aside sensitivity. You can show courage even while exposing your own sensitivity. Actually, I'd go further than that: I think it's necessary to fight to preserve your sensitivity.

Loredana Rotondo was very pleased that the play was shown in Latina, although she wasn't able to attend the performance there. It was Loredana who underlined the symbolic importance of that development in the life of the play: that the words from the city's courtroom in 1978 were spoken again in its own theatre in 2018. She spoke of this almost as a kind of transformative process that could serve as an example for the rest of Italy.

Do you think the play has stimulated reflection on how things have changed – or failed to change – in the last forty years?

This is just conjecture on my part, but I wonder if what took people by surprise was, perhaps, discovering how near to us those words seem today, despite the advances in law and societal attitudes over the forty years. It's as if, although the passage of time marks out some distance, the current relevance of that trial is readily apparent in the habits and discourses of daily life today. And I believe it's that temporal dynamic, that relationship between past and present, that allowed the play to stimulate reflection that is independent of any specific timeframe.

Beyond the telling of stories, theatre allows us to rethink words, to rethink concepts. It can make a story or a thought evoke other thoughts and stories, and I hope this is what we achieved with the play. The audience response so far has been very rewarding.

So do you feel you achieved what you set out to achieve with this play?

You know, when you create a play, a film, a book or a television programme, you hope to be able to show it to an audience, and then let yourself be surprised by the reactions to it, whatever they may be. I was surprised by the reactions that this play sparked, especially the emotional reactions. I had aimed at a distancing effect: I had sought to put some distance between past and present, in order to allow us to observe the violent behaviours that surround us, and recount them, with detachment. So the result surprised me.

And your interest in the play is itself gratifying. Yet it also speaks to me of how essential it was to carry out this project. I had not imagined it attracting attention from the other side of the world, but if it has, then it means that necessity was real.

Do you think the play will be performed again?

At the moment there are no plans for reviving the play. Although the production was created in 2018 and has had the life it has – the seasons in Rome, Latina and Cagliari, the podcast on Radio Onda Rossa (Red Wave Radio), the video screening in Australia[3] and now publication of the script in Italian and English – I think there could still be other audiences for it, because every performance generated excellent feedback, both in quantitative and qualitative terms. And the fact that we're talking about this project a few years after the performances confirms this for me. It would really be interesting to see *Processo per stupro* playing to more spectators in its theatrical form. I believe it could have useful outcomes, it could have a significant impact.

---

3 The video-recording made at the Teatro D'Annunzio in Latina in April 2018 was screened during the conference Indelible (Eng.) / *Indelebile* (It.) – Representation in the Arts of (In)visible Violence Against Women and Their Resistance, held at Flinders University in Adelaide in October 2019. The audience was provided with an earlier, unpublished translation of the play in English by Gaye Wilkinson.

References

Arcola Theatre (2014), 'BAREtruth Theatre Company. Little Stitches'. Available online: https://www.arcolatheatre.com/whats-on/little-stitches-2/ (accessed 27 August 2022).

Bellesia, G. (2000), 'Variations on a Theme: Violence Against Women in the Writings of Dacia Maraini', in R. Diaconescu-Blumenfeld and A. Testaferri (eds), *The Pleasure of Writing: Critical Essays on Dacia Maraini*, 121–34, West Lafayette: Purdue University Press.

Belmonti, M. G., A. Carini, R. Daopoulo, P. De Martiis, A. Miscuglio and L. Rotondo (1980), *Un processo per stupro: Dal programma della Rete due della televisione italiana*, preface by F. Ongaro Basaglia, Turin: Einaudi.

Breger, M. L. (2014), 'Transforming Cultural Norms of Sexual Violence Against Women', *Journal of Research in Gender Studies*, 4 (2): 39–51.

Bromley, A. K. (1992), 'Italy's New Code of Criminal Procedure (Decree of 22 September 1988, No 447)', *The Italianist*, 12, 137–78.

Buonanno, M. (2020), '*Processo per stupro*: femminismo, televisione, testimonianza', in M. Buonanno and F. Faccioli (eds), *Genere e media: non solo immagini. Soggetti, politiche, rappresentazioni*, 17–39, Milan: FrancoAngeli.

Bussoni, I. and R. Perna, eds (2014), *Il gesto femminista. La rivolta delle donne: nel corpo, nel lavoro, nell'arte*, Rome: DeriveApprodi.

Cavallaro, D. (2019), 'Changing the World with Theatre: Dacia Maraini's *Passi affrettati* in Australia', *Spunti e Ricerche*, 33: 150–68.

Cavallaro, D. (forthcoming), 'Raising Awareness of Female Genital Mutilation through Theater', *Violence Against Women*.

Cavallaro, D., L. d'Arcangeli and C. Kennedy, eds (2021), *Atti di accusa: Testi teatrali e interviste sulla rappresentazione della violenza contro le donne*, Rome: Aracne.

Coates, L., J. B. Bavelas and J. Gibson (1994), 'Anomalous Language in Sexual Assault Trial Judgments', *Discourse & Society*, 5 (2): 189–206.

Council of Europe (2011), 'Council of Europe Convention on Preventing and Combating Violence against Women and Domestic Violence'. Available online: https://rm.coe.int/168008482e (accessed 27 August 2022).

Cox, E. (2020), Personal communication with C. Kennedy, 23 May.

d'Arcangeli, L. and C. Kennedy (2022), 'Introduction. Indelible / *Indelebile*', *FULGOR*, 6 (3).

Dinos, S., N. Burrowes, K. Hammond and C. Cunliffe (2015), 'A Systematic Review of Juries' Assessment of Rape Victims: Do Rape Myths Impact on Juror Decision Making?', *International Journal of Law, Crime and Justice*, 43: 36–49.

Ehrlich, S. (2007), 'Normative Discourses and Representations of Coerced Sex', in J. Cotterill (ed.), *The Language of Sexual Crime*, 126–38, London: Palgrave Macmillan.

Equality Now (2020), 'Female Genital Mutilation/Cutting: A Call for a Global Response'. Available online: https://www.equalitynow.org/resource/female-genital-mutilation-cutting-a-call-for-a-global-response/ (accessed 27 August 2022).

Fenton, R. A. (2010), 'Rape in Italian Law: Towards the Recognition of Sexual Autonomy', in C. McGlynn and V. Munro (eds), *Rethinking Rape Law: International and Comparative Perspectives*, 183–95, London: Routledge.

Filippelli, S. (2011), 'Le ragazze con il videotape. La tv secondo Loredana Rotondo', *Bianco e nero*, 3: 97–107.

Fitzpatrick, L. (2018), *Rape on the Contemporary Stage*, London: Palgrave Macmillan.

Fontannaz, L. (2022), 'Imaging Affront, Crisis and Survival', *FULGOR*, 6 (3).

Healey V. (2015), 'Little Stitches – Omnibus, Clapham', *Theatre Bubble*, 14 April. Available online: https://www.theatrebubble.com/2015/04/little-stitches-omnibus-clapham/ (accessed 27 August 2022).

Human Rights Watch (2010), 'Q&A on Female Genital Mutilation'. Available online: https://www.hrw.org/news/2010/06/16/qa-female-genital-mutilation (accessed 27 August 2022).

ISTAT (2007), 'La violenza e i maltrattamenti contro le donne dentro e fuori la famiglia', 21 February. Available online: https://www.istat.it/it/archivio/34552 (accessed 27 August 2022).

Kay, N. (2013), '*Hurried Steps* in Performance', in D. Maraini, *Hurried Steps*, trans. S. Wood, 9, London: Camberwell Press.

Kay, N. (2014a), 'Hidden Stories, Hurried Steps: Nicolette Kay at TEDxCoventGardenWomen', 31 January. Available online: https://www.youtube.com/watch?v=C_jrwqleK-g (accessed 27 August 2022).

Kay, N. (2014b), '*Hurried Steps* Resource Pack'. Available online: https://www.hurriedsteps.org/resource-pack (accessed 27 August 2022).

Lagostena Bassi, T. (1993), 'Violence against Women and the Response of Italian Institutions', in M. Cicioni and N. Prunster (eds), *Visions and Revisions: Women in Italian Culture*, 199–212, Oxford: Berg.

Laville, S. (2015), 'Decision to Prosecute Doctor for FGM "left me with no faith in British justice"', *The Guardian*, 4 February. Available online: https://www.theguardian.com/society/2015/feb/04/prosecuting-dr-dhanuson-dharmasena-female-genital-mutilation-mistake-consultant?CMP=gu_com (accessed 27 August 2022).

Loiacono, R. (2014), 'Alcune difficoltà traduttive derivanti da una sentenza della Corte Suprema di Cassazione', *Spunti e Ricerche*, 29: 7–28.

Mandolini, N. (2018), 'Intervista a Dacia Maraini', in M. Bettaglio, N. Mandolini and S. Ross (eds), *Rappresentare la violenza di genere: Sguardi femministi tra critica, attivismo e scrittura*, 319–31, Milan: Mimesis.

Manson, C. S. (2005), 'In Love with Cecchino: Opening the Door to Violence in Dacia Maraini's *Colomba* and *Voci*', *Journal of Romance Studies*, 5 (2): 91–102.

Maraini, D. (1991), *Erzbeth Bathory; Il Geco; Norma 44*, Rome: Editori & Associati.

Maraini, D. (1994), *Mary Stuart*, in R. Helfman Kaufman (ed.), *Only Prostitutes Marry in May*, 31–124, trans. C. Pearcy with N. Kay, Toronto: Guernica.

Maraini, D. (2000), *Fare teatro (1966–2000)*, Milan: Rizzoli.

Maraini, D. (2007), *Passi affrettati*, Pescara: Ianieri.

Maraini, D. (2013), *Hurried Steps*, trans. S. Wood, London: Camberwell Press.

Neonato, S. (1992), 'Io accuso', *Noi Donne*, April, 10–16.

Pasolini, P. P. and T. Simpson (2007), 'Manifesto for a New Theatre: Pier Paolo Pasolini translated by Thomas Simpson', *PAJ: A Journal of Performance and Art*, 29 (1): 126–38.

Pedace, C. F. (2017), 'Da vittima a imputata: La violenza sessuale nel procedimento penale', *Studi sulla questione criminale*, 12 (3): 27–44.

Pitch, T. (1990), 'Rape Reform in Italy: The Endless Story', in R. Nanetti and R. Catanzaro (eds), *Italian Politics: A review*, 162–83, London: Pinter.

Plan International (2020a), 'Girls in Somalia Subjected to Door to Door FGM', 18 May. Available online: https://plan-international.org/news/2020/05/18/girls-in-somalia-subjected-to-door-to-door-fgm/ (accessed 27 August 2022).

Plan International (2020b), 'How COVID-19 Is Threatening Girls' Sexual and Reproductive Health and Rights', 29 May. Available online: https://plan-international.org/case-studies/how-covid-19-is-threatening-girls-sexual-and-reproductive-health-and-rights/ (accessed 27 August 2022).

Re, L. (2017), 'La violenza contro le donne come violazione dei diritti umani. Il ruolo dei movimenti delle donne e il *gender mainstreaming*', in G. Conte and S. Landini (eds), *Principi, regole, interpretazione: Contratti e obbligazioni, famiglie e successioni. Tomo II*, 171–85, Mantua: Universitas Studiorum.

Rogers, J. (2019), 'What Constitutes Mutilation? A Concern with Anti-Female Genital Mutilation Laws in Australia and the Question of Natural Function', *Current Sexual Health Reports*, 11 (4): 442–6.

Safi, M. (2016), 'Three Sentenced to 15 Months in Landmark Female Genital Mutilation Trial', *The Guardian*, 18 March. Available online: https://www.theguardian.com/society/2016/mar/18/three-sentenced-to-15-months-in-landmark-female-genital-mutilation-trial (accessed 27 August 2022).

Seguro, M. I. and M. Tirado (2022), 'The Crisis of Multiculturalism in Charlene James's *Cuttin' It* and Gloria Williams's *Bullet Hole*', in C. Wallace et al. (eds), *Crisis, Representation and Resilience: Perspectives on Contemporary British Theatre*, 159–74, London: Bloomsbury.

Stella, G. A. (2019), 'Violenza alle donne, il film che non possiamo vedere', *Corriere della Sera*, 26 November. Available online: https://www.corriere.it/opinioni/19_novembre_26/violenza-donne-05c44522-107d-11ea-8237-5100dbaddf11.shtml (accessed 27 August 2022).

Tompkins, J. (2014), *Theatre's Heterotopias: Performance and the Cultural Politics of Space*, London: Palgrave Macmillan.

UN Office on Drugs and Crime (2021), 'UNODC Research: 2020 Saw a Woman or Girl Being Killed by Someone in Their Family Every 11 Minutes', 25 November. Available online: https://www.unodc.org/unodc/frontpage/2021/November/unodc-research_-2020-saw-every-11-minutes-a-woman-or-girl-being-killed-by-someone-in-their-family.html (accessed 27 August 2022).

UNFPA Arab States (2018), 'FGM Performed in Clinics Can Make It Dangerously Attractive', 7 February. Available online: https://arabstates.unfpa.org/en/news/fgm-performed-clinics-can-make-it-dangerously-attractive (accessed 27 August 2022).

UNICEF (2016), 'Female Genital Mutilation/Cutting: A Global Concern', February. Available online: https://data.unicef.org/resources/female-genital-mutilationcutting-global-concern/ (accessed 27 August 2022).

United Nations General Assembly (2012), 'Intensifying Global Efforts for the Elimination of Female Genital Mutilations', A/C.3/67/L.21/Rev.1, 16 November. Available online: https://www.unfpa.org/sites/default/files/resource-pdf/67th_UNGA-Resolution_adopted_on_FGM_0.pdf (accessed 27 August 2022).

United Nations General Assembly (2020), 'Intensification of Efforts to Eliminate All Forms of Violence against Women and Girls. Report of the Secretary-General', A/75/274, 30 July. Available online: https://undocs.org/en/A/75/274 (accessed 27 August 2022).

UN WOMEN (n. d.), 'Violence against Women. Work of the General Assembly on Violence against Women'. Available online: https://www.un.org/womenwatch/daw/vaw/reports.htm (accessed 27 August 2022).

UN WOMEN (2015), 'Beijing Declaration and Platform for Action, Beijing +5 Political Declaration and Outcome'. Available online: https://www.unwomen.org/en/digital-library/publications/2015/01/beijing-declaration (accessed 27 August 2022).

WHO (2022), 'Female Genital Mutilation – Fact Sheet'. Available online: https://www.who.int/news-room/fact-sheets/detail/female-genital-mutilation (accessed 27 August 2022).

Willis, E. (2021), *Metatheatrical Dramaturgies of Violence: Staging the Role of Theatre*, London: Palgrave Macmillan.

Willson, P. (2010), *Women in Twentieth-Century Italy*, New York: Palgrave Macmillan.

Wood, S. (2013), 'Translation and the Performative Text: Dacia Maraini's *Passi affrettati*', in A. De Martino, P. Puppa and P. Toninato (eds), *Differences on Stage*, 191–206, Newcastle upon Tyne: Cambridge Scholars Publishing.

World Bank (2022), 'Women, Business and the Law 2022'. Available online: https://wbl.worldbank.org/en/wbl (accessed 27 August 2022).